THE GUIDE TO

Good Eating

In Lincoln Land and Central Illinois

by Susan Taylor

Cover design and illustrations
by Susan Bostic Stockton

Fifth Sin Press

P.O. Box 4133 Springfield, IL 62708

To Stephen, my partner in love, politics, and culinary pursuits
and to Danny, my source of indescribable joy.

Introduction

Just about everyone loves good food. Whether you live in an area or are just visiting, finding the right restaurant--the one that serves good food with fresh ingredients cooked to order from scratch--makes the experience all the more pleasurable. And nothing makes a better souvenir or present than a gift of food from the culinary bounty where you live or visit.

Every area has its own unique culinary bounty. When I moved to Springfield from Chicago six years ago, I really had no idea what it meant to live among some of the world's richest farmland. In deciding to write this book, I embarked on a process of discovery. I have been surprised and delighted by what I found in this land known only for corn and soybeans. Here in central Illinois you can buy Thomas Jefferson's favorite apple--and a hundred other varieties. Here in our backyard, we can pick fresh pecans from the largest pecan grove this far north in America. We can buy organic, free-range chicken from the farm or eat that chicken in a restaurant in Urbana. We can pick fresh strawberries for making jam or have those strawberries in a dessert at a beautiful restaurant that serves superb beef. Fresh asparagus, morel mushrooms, raspberries, local cheese--they are all here. And the list doesn't stop there. Here in the land of industrial agriculture you can find ripe from the tree peaches, nectarines, and plums; farm-fresh melons and produce; award-winning Amish cheese, local maple syrup, and local honey harvested from soybeans.

But is bounty enough? No, we need good restaurants--and we have them. They are in Springfield, Champaign, Urbana, Bloomington, and Decatur. They are in Arcola, Tuscola, Dalton City, and Casey. They are in Jacksonville, Naples, Meredosia, and Kampsville. They are in Monticello, Oakland, Sullivan, Taylorville, Pana, and Paris. In Central Illinois you can find wonderful Mexican food. You can eat fresh catfish while you watch the Illinois river from the porch of a restored mansion. You can be transported from Paris, Illinois, to Paris,

France, by dining on superb classic French cuisine in a converted fast-food restaurant. You can eat creative, country-style cooking in an old dairy barn that has been transformed into a beautiful, garden-laden restaurant. In Springfield, you can eat a huge, southern-style breakfast for a pittance and dinner from the kitchen of the chef who is creating a unique heartland cuisine with local wild mushrooms, asparagus, watercress, and garden-grown produce and herbs. Yet I am saddened by the loss of four restaurants that I had planned to include in this book. Small restaurants serving inexpensive food and without large budgets for advertising are obviously the most vulnerable. So if you like a restaurant, don't go there once every six months. Tell your friends, and go more often--or it might not be there when you go back.

In writing this book, I did not try to rate restaurants. Some of the restaurants that I included are excellent, some are good, and a few are simply "on the road" alternatives to fast food or a good place to stop for something in particular. Read the restaurant descriptions carefully, and if you're in an area without a recommended restaurant, check the map in the front of the book, and go to one of the restaurants nearby--some are definitely worth a drive. I apologize to the few good restaurants that I didn't have time to review and hope to include them in a future edition of this book. I also welcome readers comments and suggestions.

I hope you will use this book to inspire you to discover the area. When you go to the wonderful Little Theatre on the Square in Sullivan, eat at Jibby's, stop at the local bakery for eclairs, and if the season is right pick strawberries. Plan a trip to New Salem during blueberry season and on the way there pick berries and stop for a cool beer on the patio of a Mexican restaurant in Pleasant Plains. Dance under the stars at the corn and bean festival in Oakland after eating French cuisine in nearby Paris, and the next day take your kids to pick pumpkins, play in a straw maze, and go on a haunted hay ride, and stop for apples at a nearby apple orchard. In Amish country, take home some award-winning cheese from Arthur's master cheesemakers, and eat whoopie pies from an Amish bakery. On your way to the annual antique show in Bloomington in March, make a side trip to Shirley for maple syrup and show your kids how maple syrup is made. These are just a few of the ideas this book will give you to help you experience the culinary bounty of central Illinois.

This book is organized in two sections. Both sections are organized alphabetically by town. The first section, *Restaurants, Bakeries, and Shops,* lists restaurants first alphabetically and then lists the shops alphabetically. The second section, *Farm-Fresh Products,* lists the orchards, farms, and groves alphabetically. Within the second section you will also find a chart of apple varieties, a list of taverns that sell morel mushrooms in season, and an assortment of mail-order food businesses.

I have attempted to give you a general idea of the cost of meals at restaurants. Please understand that prices change, but I expect that the basic categories, within a dollar or two, will remain fairly stable. Restaurants that I call *inexpensive* serve meals for less than $6.00. Those that are *moderate* serve meals priced from $6.00 to $12.00. *Moderately expensive* is a meal priced between $12.00 to $18.00, and *expensive* is one that is more than $18.00.

Thanks

Much of the work of researching, writing, and putting together this book was fun because of the enthusiastic support of a number of people. Special thanks to Karen Hewitt, my editor, who was a constant source of encouragement, information, and professional expertise, and to Susan Stockton for her beautiful illustrations and cover design.

I am grateful to the farmers, orchardists, beekeepers, and cheesemakers who helped this city girl understand and appreciate some of what it takes to create this rich, agricultural bounty. Thanks to the bakers and chefs who work long, hard hours to give us so much more than mere sustenance. Thanks to Nancy Howard Higgins for helping me learn about the food business. Thanks to Brent Bohlen for providing me with information about apples, and to Southmeadow Fruit Gardens, whose catalog was a valuable source of information on apple varieties. Special thanks to the ACF Central Illinois Culinary Arts Association for providing scholarships to local chefs.

I was able to work on this book because I knew that my son, Danny, was being well cared for by the teachers and staff of the Revenue Child Development Center: My sincere appreciation to Kelley Wilson, Sharon Folkerts, Julie Zgaga, Linda Voltz, and to the rest of the staff for helping Danny to love to learn. Thanks to Alan and Paul Whitaker who helped me work my way through the maze of computer terminology.

During the period I worked on this book, two people who were very dear to me died: Frederick Spence and Greg Noriega are remembered lovingly in these pages. Thanks to my precious Danny for trying new foods and for thinking that Daddies make pies and Mommies carry notebooks to write about food. Most of all, I am grateful to my husband, Stephen Spence, who was always there--whether I was driving him across the prairie to another restaurant, unloading a trunk full of food for him to taste at 11:00 p.m., or listening to my middle-of-the-night misgivings--for his unwavering support and encouragement.

Contents

Restaurants, Bakeries, and Shops

Farm-Fresh Products

Lincoln
Kasa's Produce 101, Ott's Honey 102, Three Sisters Orchard and Greenhouse 102

Mahomet
Twin Silos Orchard (berries, apples, grapes) 102

Melvin
Second Nature Farm (organic chickens) 103

Moweaqua
Bohlen's Orchard 104

New Berlin
Buckman's Orchard   104, Spring Creek Farm (organic eggs and poultry) 105

Pana
White Oak Farm (organic beef and produce) 105

Petersburg
The Shirding Farm (asparagus) 106

Pleasant Plains
Fromm-Huff Farm (blueberries) 107

Pontiac
Jones Strawberry Woods (berries and pumpkins) 107

Rochester
Carol Harp (herbs) 108, Cascade Sheep and Wool Company 108

Sadorus
Herbs of Grace 109

San Jose
Clark's Greenhouse and Herbal Country 109

Shirley
Funks Grove (maple sirup) 110

Map of Central Illinois

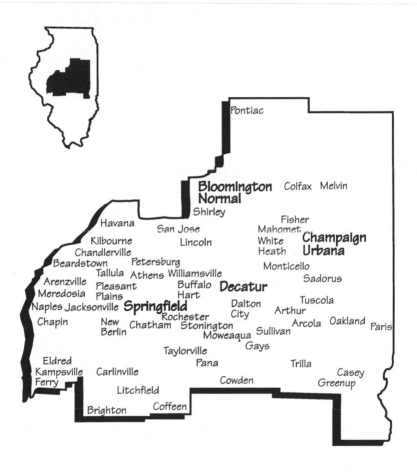

Restaurants Bakeries & Shops

Arcola

The Dutch Kitchen Restaurant
127 E. Main
(217) 268-3518
Open: Daily
7:30 a.m.-7:00 p.m.
Price range: Inexpensive

The Dutch Kitchen serves good, if undistinguished, Amish home-style cooking. Ham and eggs, biscuits, and apple butter are typical of what's available for breakfast. For lunch or dinner there is Dutch sausage, chicken, roast beef, ham and beans, catfish, and soup and sandwiches on the list of menu items.

The broasted chicken is deep-fried and good. It is served with smooth mashed potatoes and creamy white gravy, tasty bread dressing, and a vegetable. The green beans flavored with bacon are savory but overcooked. The homemade bread is dull and is served with apple butter. The Dutch sausage has a mild smoked flavor. An Amish specialty, the shoo-fly pie served here has a flaky crust but an unfortunately bland filling flavored mainly with cinnamon.

The French Embassy
Rt. 133
(217) 268-4949 or 268-4940
Open: Tuesday through Saturday
5:00 p.m.-9:00 p.m.
Price Range: Moderate to expensive
Reservations recommended

Although the bowling alley came first, the restaurant's name is apt, for what introduces one culture to another better than food? The "ambassador" of the French Embassy is Chef Jean-Louis Ledent, originally from Belgium. Ledent trained in

Europe and cooked there for many years before moving to the U.S. Visitors to Amish country should not pass up the unique opportunity to eat at this restaurant, which has been the recent focus of national publicity due to its unusual location in a bowling alley. Fun-loving types can reserve a lane for bowling and a table later for dinner, but don't worry, the crash of bowling pins can't be heard in the tranquil dining room.

While the menu changes every six months, many of the same items remain. There is a fixed-price four-course meal that changes every four or five days, or you may compose your own meal from a large selection of appetizers, entrees of beef, lamb, poultry, pork, or seafood, and desserts. Some of the items on the menu are excellent, and while others were disappointing, it is possible to have a wonderful meal here.

A regular offering is the fish soup, a thick puree with an intense fish flavor--not for the timid, it is a very good choice for the adventurous. A good chicken liver paté, served with chopped onion and toast is nicely presented with decorative slices of seasonal fruits, vegetables, and fresh herb sprigs. The French onion soup, a bowl of beef-based soup with onions, is disappointing, as is the *coquilles St. Jacques au champagne* (scallops in champagne cream sauce), which would be quite good if the fish stock used in the sauce weren't too salty. Other appetizer possibilities include Norwegian smoked salmon with chopped onions and frozen vodka, stuffed pastry with poached snails in a Riesling cream sauce, and poached frog legs in a creamy spinach sauce. The house salad, a basic salad of iceberg lettuce, is served with two dressings, which are brought to the table. The house dressing is a sweet, mayonnaise and tomato-based dressing, and the viniagrette is tart and tangy with lots of herbs.

An excellent entree is the sauteed lamb with garlic and green beans (sometimes other vegetables, such as artichokes, will be paired with the lamb) in a white Bordeaux wine sauce. The perfectly cooked (medium-rare) chunks of lamb sauteed with garlic and onions are tender and delicious, and the green beans are fresh and not overcooked; the white Bordeaux sauce is a perfect complement to the lamb and vegetables. A nice, simple entree is the charbroiled chicken breast flavored with herbs and fresh lemon juice. The chicken breast is marinated in the lemon juice and herbs before it is grilled, making it tender, juicy, and flavorful. The French-fried potatoes served alongside the chicken are thin and crispy. Sweetbreads, properly prepared, are an unusual treat. Here, the large portion of very good sweetbreads is baked in a rich beef-based cream sauce and served with whole mushrooms. A delicious side dish of au gratin potatoes is rich with butter and cheese. A potentially interesting but disappointing entree is the baked quails with bacon and onions. Juniper berries add the flavor of gin, which stands up well to the powerful flavor of bacon, but unfortunately the quail is a bit dry and the rice served with the dish is dull. Filet mignon, a very popular entree at the restaurant, is served with a choice of four sauces: bearnaise, mushroom cream, green peppercorn, or three pepper (black, white, and green) cream. Other interesting entrees include sauteed chicken breast with five-herb cream sauce, sauteed veal filet mignon with sage cream sauce, sauteed pork filet mignon with a choice of chopped onions and red Bordeaux wine sauce or Dijon mustard sauce, and charbroiled shrimp kabob on a bed of carrot, celery, onion, and leek julienne. A daily fish special is also available.

The French Embassy serves some very good desserts. The creme brulee is a creamy baked custard with a crunchy topping of broiled brown sugar. The pear cake with warm chocolate sauce is a single layer moist yellow cake with chunks of pear; it is served with an excellent bittersweet chocolate sauce. The same delicious chocolate is used in the dark chocolate mousse-- a dense mousse flavored with a hint of cherry. The coffee is served with chocolate coffee beans. The restaurant has a basic wine list.

Main St. Deli
201 E. Main St.
(217) 268-4821
Open: Daily
8:00 a.m.-5:00 p.m. weekdays (Thursday and Friday until 8:00
p.m)
9:00 a.m.-8:00 p.m. Saturday and 4:00 p.m.-8:00 p.m. Sunday
Price Range: Inexpensive

An alternative to heavy home-style cooking is the deli fare found at the Main St. Deli. This little restaurant in the Arcola Emporium serves typical deli foods, including salads, soups, and sandwiches stuffed with cold cuts, cheeses, or meat and seafood salads. The creamy turkey salad with carrots and almonds is a nice choice. The deli has a small selection of items with a listing of their calorie count for the calorie conscious. For those not dieting, there are various cookies and such decadent selections as chocolate truffle mousse, pumpkin praline cheesecake, and carrot cake. The peanut butter blossom cookies are very good, and the lemon cookies are light and lemony. A selection of baked goods to go, including some Amish items, is available. The whole wheat bread is light and chewy.

The Arcola Pharmacy
102-104 E. Main St.
(217) 268-3636
Open: Monday through Saturday
8:00 a.m.-5:00 p.m. except Saturday until 2:30 p.m.

The Arcola Pharmacy was made famous by Charles Kuralt, who did a spot on its unusual coffee club for his "On the Road" TV series. The old-fashioned soda fountain sells coke (and cherry and lemon-flavored coke) in glass coke glasses, as well ice cream sundaes, sodas, malts, shakes, cones, and percolated coffee. The woman behind the counter makes a good malt. But the main reason tourists come to see the pharmacy is to see the coffee mugs of the members of "Arrol's Coffee Club." Each of the 162 members has a cubby hole holding a mug with the member's name. Each member drank 100 cups of coffee and waited on a waiting list in order to become a member of the club. Drinking 100 cups of this coffee is not difficult. It is fresh coffee, made in an old-fashioned percolator, and served with a tiny glass bottle of half-and-half. This is a fun place to show your kids what an old-fashioned soda-fountain was like and to have a good cup of coffee.

The Cook's Collection
201 E. Main St.
(217) 268-3311
Open: Every day
9:00 a.m.-5:00 p.m. (Sunday 12:00 p.m.-5:00 p.m.)

This shop is located in the Arcola Emporium. It has a very useful selection of kitchenware, cooking gadgets, and gourmet specialty foods.

Arthur

The Arthur Cheese Company
P.O. Box 308
(217) 543-2166
Open: Monday through Saturday
8:00 a.m.-5:00 p.m. (Saturday until 4:00 p.m.)

The Arthur Cheese Company produces wonderful natural cheese. The Baby Swiss won first place in the U.S. Cheesemakers' Association competition in 1987 and third place in the organization's 1990 worldwide competition; it was the only U.S. cheese to place in the top 10, and it is a wonderful creamy cheese. Cheddar, smoked cheddar, Gouda, and low-fat Swiss are among other delicious selections from the 30 or so produced by the company. Samples are available at the shop, so you can taste a number of varieties before choosing which to buy. Please note: the award-winning Baby Swiss is called Danish Swiss on the price list.

The shop, which is attached to the factory, also sells sausages, preserves, condiments, crackers, breads, and novelty items such as wax-coated pig-and cow-shaped cheeses, which make good Christmas-stocking stuffers. Cheeses can be purchased at the shop or by mail-order. A gift catalog, with various cheese assortments, is also available on request. (See *Mail-Order Shopping* for mailing address.)

Beachy's Eggs and Produce
R. R. 1, Box 18
Open: Monday through Saturday
7:00 a.m.-6:00 p.m. (Saturday until 4:00 p.m.)

Beachy's has grown beyond its name and is, in fact, an unusual grocery store, lit by propane lamps on the ceiling. It has an attached kitchen from which Amish women produce many of the products for sale in the store. Among the homemade items are egg noodles, jams and jellies, candies, and a line of bakery products including bread, angel food cakes, cinnamon rolls, cookies, whoopie pies, and more. Beachy's also stocks fresh produce, fresh white and brown eggs, and a large selection of bulk foods including nuts, grains, and spices.

Some of the homemade items are quite good. The miniature dill bread containing cottage cheese, dill seed, minced onion, and butter is a moist, herbal loaf. The egg noodles are first rate. Black raspberry jam, made with fruit at its peak flavor, is a real treat. Sweet and gooey pecan rolls are loaded with pecans. Angel food cakes come in assorted flavors: strawberry, vanilla, apricot, blackberry, and chocolate chip; the cakes are moist and tasty. Beachy's makes a very popular specialty item called a whoopie pie. It looks like an oreo cookie cake--two cookie-sized dark chocolate cakes held together by white icing. They are a special treat for children.

Family Health Foods
R.R. 1 Box 129
Monday through Saturday
8:00 a.m.-5:00 p.m. (Saturday until 4:00 p.m.)

This health food store, lit by skylights and propane lamps, has an unusual selection of bulk foods. In addition to herbs, spices, nuts, dried fruits, chocolate, carob, beans, and pastas, this store stocks hard-to-find bulk flours such as oat, barley, buckwheat, graham, dark rye, corn meal, and semolina. It has juices, honey, sorghum, and candy flavorings along with a varied selection of candies, including caramels, carob stars, cashew clusters, sugar-free carob coconut clusters, carob maltballs, and yogurt maltballs. The homemade caramels, made with cream and butter, are rich, smooth, and delicious. The store also carries "healthy" cosmetics.

Miller's Bakery
Rt. 133 (past Chesterville, R.R. Arthur)
Open: Monday through Saturday
8:00 a.m.-4:30 p.m (4:00 Saturday)

You might have to walk through pecking chickens to get to Miller's Bakery. This Amish establishment produces bread, cookies, cinnamon rolls, angel food cakes, noodles, and hard candies, including cough drops that really work. The white bread is dull, but the cinnamon rolls are good, moist and spicy. A sign says that fresh cream is available. When asked, a young woman will disappear into the house across from the bakery and reemerge a few minutes later with a recycled jar filled with heavy cream that has undoubtedly just been spooned from the top of fresh milk. This cream is a real treat.

Bloomington and Normal

Nuevo Chimi's Caribbean and Mexican Cuisine
503 N. Prospect
Bloomington
(309) 662-9607
Open: Monday through Saturday
11:00 a.m.-9:00 p.m. (4:00 p.m.-10:00 p.m. Saturday)
Price range: Inexpensive

Nuevo Chimi's is a simple, storefront restaurant that serves good Mexican and Caribbean specialties. It has the usual Mexican dishes such as tacos, enchiladas, burritos, and tamales, as well as harder to find *chile rellenos* and Caribbean-style stews, steaks, chicken, and shrimp. There is a nice selection of appetizers. A very good choice for an appetizer is the *frijoles con chorizo,* a large bowl of refried beans mixed with spicy chorizo sausage, onions, tomatoes, peppers, and spices, and topped with gooey melted cheese. *Platano,* the fried banana-like fruit, is another menu item. Ask for sweet (ripe) platanos, which are a real treat; you might find the green ones too starchy and bland.

The enchiladas are tasty and the chile rellenos, cheese-stuffed, breaded, and deep-fried poblano peppers, are surprisingly spicy, but very good. The accompanying refried beans and rice are also good. *Pollo de Campo*, a large portion of marinated and grilled chicken that is served in a tomato-based sauce with green peppers and onions, is an unusual and satisfying dish. There are steaks and hamburgers for the timid. You can cool off your palate with a domestic or imported beer, or heat things up with a Puerto Rican Fizz, a Haitian Hurricane, or a more sedate cocktail.

Phil's Bar and Grill
401 N. Veterans Parkway (in the Eastland Mall)
Bloomington
(309) 662-9637
Open: Monday through Saturday
11:00 a.m.-2:00 p.m. and 5:00 p.m.-9:30 p.m. (until 10:30 Friday and Saturday) and not open for lunch on Saturday
Price range: Moderate to moderately expensive
Reservations recommended on weekends

Skeptics who say that you can't get excellent seafood in central Illinois haven't been to Phil's. Tucked away in the same nondescript shopping mall as Cub Foods is the best fish and seafood restaurant in central Illinois. Once inside the oak-decorated restaurant, you will quickly forget the exterior. Fresh seafood is the mainstay of this restaurant, but creatively prepared steaks, lamb chops, ribs, and rotisserie-roasted items are also available. For lunch, you can choose from fish or pasta specials, or try such menu items as scallop melt on an English muffin; chicken, avocado, and bacon sandwich, served open-faced with bernaise sauce; Phil's special two-cabbage pork sandwich; or you can choose from among a variety of salads and appetizers.

The blackboard at the entrance lists the day's specials. Delicious gumbo is thick and chock-full of chicken, sausage, and shrimp; spinach and scallop soup nicely combine earthy and delicate flavors; and black bean and steak chili is an intriguing possibility. Some of the most creative cooking is evident in the appetizers: a delicious shrimp special combines chunks of fresh mozzarella with spicy sausage slices and shrimp in a sauce of balsamic vinegar and basil; a simple appetizer of smoked salmon cakes with red pepper and onion bits is very satisfying; and mild and meaty deep-fried grouper fingers with dill sauce are a nice selection. A better-than-average salad has some interesting dressing possibilities; the house ranch dressing with bacon is too sweet but the vinaigrette has lots of herbs and a fresh, tangy flavor, and the garlic dressing is very creamy and very garlicky.

While some of the entrees at Phil's are excellent, others are disappointing. Charbroiled salmon is not on the menu, but this excellent choice is listed almost every day as a lunch or dinner special. The large fresh filet is perfectly cooked and served in a tarragon-spiked bernaise sauce, which nicely complements the rich delicate fish. A special of pan-fried mahi-mahi rolled in a macadamia nut breading is rich and flavorful. Unfortunately, the fresh swordfish was marinated too long in a soy-based marinade, giving it an unpleasantly strong, salty taste, and the shrimp and garlic fettuccini has tough shrimp and an odd-tasting pasta. Offered too are lobster tails, crab, and shrimp; you can also order them in combinations with prime rib, steak, or BBQ ribs.

For dessert there are some excellent possibilities. The marjolaine is composed of layers of white and dark chocolate that is rich and truffle-like, sandwiched between walnut cake that has been flavored with a hint of Kahlua. The result is a complex, but not confusing, combination of flavors. A chocolate mousse cake with chocolate-wafer crust and rich, dense mousse is the choice for chocolate lovers who do not care to have other flavors interfere with their chocolate. Phil's has a small wine list with many good values.

Common Ground Natural Foods
516 N. Main St.
Bloomington 61701
(309) 829-2621
Open: Monday through Saturday
9:30 a.m.-5:30 p.m.

The Common Ground has a nice selection of fresh organic produce in addition to the usual nonperishable items found in health food stores. Here, you can find bulk items such as cereals, nuts, seeds, dried fruits, pastas, herbs, spices, raw sugars, sea salt, grains, rices, beans, and lentils. Also available are packaged items such as oils, vinegars, peanut butter, cookies, cereals, juices, and teas. A refrigerator contains eggs, cheese, yogurt, soy products, cheeses, breads, butter, margarine and tofu. Body care products and vitamin supplements can be purchased.

Cotter's Bakery
422 N. Main St.
Bloomington
(309) 829-2023
Open: Monday through Saturday
5:30 a.m.-4:30 p.m. (Saturday until noon)

Cotter's is an old-fashioned family-owned and operated bakery offering inexpensive breads, cookies, pies, donuts, Danish pastries, brownies, and cakes. The pumpernickel bread is great, and the wheat bread is very good. White, dark rye, raisin, and Vienna breads are also available. Cotter's has a large assortment of pretty little party cookies. Especially good are the peanut butter swirls, Mexican wedding cakes, buckeyes, and the chocolate-covered macaroons. The large chocolate chip and the peanut butter cookies are also good. The biggest surprise are the fruit pies. Most bakery fruit pies have tough crust and more filling than fruit in the pie. Not Cotters' pies: Their crust is tender and flaky and the cherry and apple fillings are full of fruit. The fruit pie selection varies daily. Cotter's also has a take-out lunch counter serving soups, sandwiches and Chicago-style hot dogs.

The Garlic Press
108 North St.
Normal
(309) 452-8841
Open: Monday through Saturday
10:00 a.m.-5:30 p.m. (Saturday 9:30 a.m.-5:30 p.m.)

The Garlic Press, an exceptionally nice kitchen and gourmet specialty shop, is an excellent place to shop for gifts for people of all ages. In addition to carefully selected kitchen and serving items, it has a good selection of creative children's toys and books. The Garlic Press carries Rubens Chocolates, an outstanding brand of locally produced fine Belgian chocolates. You can buy these chocolates individually or in elegant gold boxes. Be sure to try the excellent traditional truffles, the heavenly butter giandujas (hazelnut-cream-filled chocolates) and the liquid-gold honey caramels (white chocolate filled with runny caramel sweetened with honey). This shop also has a very good selection of cookbooks, kitchen gadgets, cutlery, and handmade jewelry.

Casey

Richard's Farm Restaurant
R.R. 1
(217) 932-5300
Open: Daily
Monday through Sunday 11:00 a.m.-1:30 p.m. and 5:30 p.m.-
8:30 p.m. (until 9:30 p.m. Friday and Saturday)
Price range: Moderate to moderately expensive

Richard's Farm serves home-style cooking at its creative best. But it is not for the cooking alone that customers have been driving, since 1976, to this restaurant in the middle of nowhere. The restaurant and the garden-laden approach to it are lovely. Housed in a hip-roof barn built in the 1930s, Richard's Farm has an enchanting vine-covered entrance, a wooden interior, and lanterns, ropes, and butter churns to remind you of its origin.

The onion-loaf appetizer is a loaf-shaped mountain of crispy deep-fried sweet onions. Brought to the table piping hot, they are delicious. The salad, soup, and bread bar has the usual assortment of tossed salad ingredients, as well as pasta, potato, and cucumber salad, and cole slaw, cottage cheese, and tapioca. The hearty vegetable soup is loaded with fresh vegetables, barley, and herbs. Outstanding homemade strawberry preserves and excellent spicy apple butter accompany the cut-your-own loaves of fresh-baked white, wheat, and cinnamon swirl bread that are available at the salad bar.

Richard's Farm is famous for its one-pound pork chop, which is the specialty of the house. People with less than a gargantuan appetite can order a half-pound version of the chop. It is roasted for three hours and then broiled in a special B-B-Q sauce, which is also served on the side. Although it tasted wonderful, the pork chop was a bit dry. The fried chicken does not suffer the same fate: it is as fried chicken should be--crispy on the outside, moist and tender on the inside. Served with hearty green beans cooked with bacon and onions, and creamy mashed potatoes and brown gravy, this special of the day is very satisfying.

The menu features a nice selection of six items for children. The kid's hamburger is grilled over coals made of hickory, sassafrass, and other hardwoods, giving it an unusual smoked flavor. Lots of fries accompany the burger, which is served on a sesame seed bun.

Richard's Farm has homemade desserts that fit the season. The peach cobbler a la mode is outstanding. Enough for two dessert lovers, the cobbler is loaded with perfectly ripe peaches with just the right amount of sugar to give it a sweet-tart flavor. The substantial crust topping the peaches is very good; the cobbler is served with rich vanilla ice cream. The menu also lists fruit pies of the season and an unusual persimmon pudding. Richard's Farm has a small selection of wines.

Champaign and Urbana

The Blind Pig
6 Taylor St. (brick plaza downtown)
Champaign
(217) 351-7444
Open: Monday through Saturday (music daily)
11:00 a.m.-3:00 p.m.

The Blind Pig is about as funky a place as you are likely to find in central Illinois, which is too bad--we need more places like this! A changing collection of original paintings and a cluster of small tables covered with bright, floral plastic tablecloths are gathered in the front room of this music bar that features interesting live music almost every night of the week. When the weather is mild, tables are set up outside. Unfortunately they can't serve liquor outside because they are using city property.

The food here is fresh and often exciting. Each day one or two special salads and soups are listed. Special sandwiches or other entrees may also be featured. The menu lists a small selection of sandwich fillings with your choice of a large variety of condiments and two types of nice, fresh bread. You can mix and match soups, salads, and sandwiches to get just the size lunch you want. The Blind Pig offers desserts from Sweet Indulgence, a local bakery, as well as a large selection of domestic and imported beers.

The Bread Company
625 E. Green
Champaign
(217) 344-2112
Open: Monday through Saturday
8:30 a.m.-7:00 p.m. (until 6:00 p.m. Saturday)
Price range: Inexpensive

The Bread Company is a good place to buy freshly baked bread or to have a sandwich made with your choice from among six types of bread. The French bread is crispy outside and chewy and substantial inside. The *zupfke*, an egg twist bread similar to *challah*, is tasty but does not have the smooth elasticity of good challah. The hearty rye bread has a nice sour flavor with a dense, moist texture and crispy, chewy crust. The whole wheat bread is moist and surprisingly light with a crispy crust. The croissants, although tasty, are not light and flaky as good croissants should be. The Bread Company is a busy place for lunch, during which time it serves deli sandwiches, soups, and cookies and pastries.

The Courier Cafe
111 N. Race St.
Urbana
(217) 328-1811
Open: Daily
7:00 a.m.-midnight

Tucked into a corner building just off Main St. in Urbana, this popular restaurant offers wholesome food in pleasant surroundings. Since it is busy morning, noon, and night, you may find a long line of people ahead of you. Named after the newspaper that used to be housed in this building, the Courier Cafe carries the theme into the menu selections--most particularly with the ice cream treats. You can order your choice of five types of sundae, from the Headliner or the Red Hot Story to the Misprint. The cafe also makes hand-dipped shakes in all fountain flavors, plus phosphates, floats, and New York egg creams.

For breakfast the very hungry can choose from various egg, meat, and bread combinations as well as from French toast, pancakes, or omelettes, and the less hungry can order toast or pastries baked fresh on the premises. At lunch you'll find 14 different sandwich offerings, some of which are vegetarian, and an additional seven types of special burgers, which can be ordered with the Courier's interesting sweet potato fries. The dinner menu is basic: steak, fried chicken, shrimp, or clams. A light alternative might be oven-baked trout. The fried chicken is crispy with a nicely seasoned batter and moist, flavorful meat. Dinner entrees come with a trip to the salad bar plus your choice of potato or rice and a homemade wheat roll. The salad bar has an impressive array of fresh fruits, vegetables, and prepared salads, and several unusual dressings. The salad bar is open for lunch, too.

A children's menu offers low-priced meals that include an entree, fries, kid-friendly salads (applesauce or cottage cheese), and a small sundae. Or you can order special sandwiches geared toward children's tastes.

The Embassy
114 S. Race
Urbana
(217) 384-9526
Open: Monday through Saturday
11:00 a.m.-11:00 p.m.
Price range: Inexpensive

When it's a hamburger you crave, the Embassy is a good place to go for an inexpensive grilled burger. Be sure to order the grilled onions with your hamburger at this tavern with a grill. The large, thin, "fall-off-the-bun" type burger, smothered in golden-grilled onions, is served on a sesame seed bun with chips. The menu has other sandwiches as well as daily specials such as ribeye steak or B-B-Q pork sandwiches.

Espresso Royale Cafe
1117 W. Oregon
Urbana (217) 337-6160
602 E. Daniel
Champaign (217) 328-1112
Open: Daily
6:30 a.m.-midnight

Enjoy a continental breakfast or stop in during the day for a relaxing cup of espresso or cappuccino at either of the two Espresso Royale locations. High quality fresh coffee, properly roasted and brewed, provides coffee lovers with the real thing. In addition to hot coffee specialties, including espresso, cappuccino, cafe con leche, and cafe mocha, there are non-coffee hot drinks such as hot almond milk, hot chocolate, and hot honey and milk. Cold drinks include iced cafe mocha, iced regular coffee, Italian or French sodas, iced tea, lemonade, and fresh orange juice. Espresso Royale has good scones and an interesting selection of pastries such as croissants, muffins, fruit and nut breads, brownies, and cheesecakes.

The Great Impasta
132 W. Church St.
Champaign
(217) 359-7377
Open: Daily
9:30 a.m.-10:00 p.m.
Price Range: Moderate

The Great Impasta is a cheerful and bustling restaurant. All the pastas, sauces, soups, and salads served at the Great Impasta are made from scratch. The pastas here are not the transparent and delicate type; instead, they are chewy and hearty. The restaurant has a small breakfast menu and a Sunday brunch but most people come for lunch and dinner. Appetizers, a large selection of all-vegetable salads or pasta-and-vegetable salads, traditional pasta dishes, as well as soups and sandwiches are all available. A number of items on the menu fall within the dietary recommendations of the American Heart Association and are designated with a heart symbol. The Great Impasta offers a few wines.

An unusual selection of pasta dishes, many of which are variations on traditional pasta recipes, is one reason for this restaurant's popularity. You can have traditional-style lasagna with tomato and bechamel sauce, or you can try seafood lasagna made with spinach noodles and layered with shrimp and crabmeat. Meat or spinach-and-cheese ravioli is served with your choice of a traditional tomato sauce, a creamy Gorgonzola (blue cheese) sauce, or an Alfredo sauce. For something a little different there is shrimp and feta cheese *a la Greque*; in this dish spaghetti noodles are tossed with very plump, fresh shrimp, chunks of feta cheese, black and green olive slices, and vegetables in a light, herbed-parmesan sauce. Other interesting pasta dishes include *linguine ai frutti di mare* (linguine with shrimp, scallops, and crabmeat in a cream sauce); white and spinach fettuccine tossed with prosciutto, mushrooms, and peas in cream sauce; and spaghetti with a tomato-based clam sauce. For dessert the Great Impasta has ice cream and a variety of cakes, pies, and tarts from Sweet

Indulgence, a local bakery. You can view the pastries in the case near the cash register. And they are a sight to see! Six types of chocolate cake that are indeed rich and indulgent are not, unfortunately, very different from one another. Everything can be ordered to go, including freshly made pasta, which you can take home to cook with your own special sauce.

Silvercreek
402 N. Race
Urbana
(217) 328-3402
Open: Daily
11:00 a.m.-10:00 p.m. (Sunday 10:30 a.m.-3:00 p.m. and 5:00 p.m.-10:00 p.m)
Price range: Moderate to moderately expensive

Silvercreek is a very pretty restaurant decorated with lots of polished wood, fireplaces, brass chandeliers, and beautiful flower arrangements. The extensive menu is filled with innovative sauces and spicy variations on common dishes, as well as simpler items for the less adventurous; the execution, however, is sometimes uneven. The many ways in which the restaurant tries hard to please are evident in such touches as the dinner salad with its nice assortment of fresh vegetables and a selection of interesting dressings such as ginger-mustard, and the fresh warm rolls that are baked on the premises. Some of the most innovative food is found in the appetizer section. A sampler plate allows you to try a variety of these tidbits: fresh mushroom caps are stuffed with chopped fresh vegetables, herbs, and brown rice, giving them a chewy texture; cayenne Bermuda onions, thinly sliced and dipped in a very peppery batter before being deep-fried, are good but become unpleasantly soggy if not eaten when hot; crispy tortilla-breaded chicken fingers have a wonderful corn-cumin flavor and are served with a spicy poblano chili sauce; delicious jumbo shrimp are rolled in coconut and fried, which gives them a slightly sweet flavor, and served with a tangy pineapple-ginger sauce; and delicately spiced, seafood-filled phyllo triangles are served on top of a sauce made of pasilla peppers that impart an intense paprika flavor. Daily soup specials continue the innovative trend; the eggplant chicken soup, loaded with fresh vegetables, chicken, and rosemary is good but a bit too vinegary.

Silvercreek has some interesting pasta dishes. Pasta Liguria combines the intense flavor of sun-dried tomatoes with the delicate flavor of leeks and the earthy tastes of spinach and mushrooms in a beef-stock based sauce. The freshly shredded cheese that tops the dish is a bit too bland, but this pasta combination works well. Other pasta entrees include one made with three types of mushrooms and three types of cheeses, and a chicken and artichoke pasta. Chicken Marabella is a large serving of half a chicken that has been marinated in olive oil, wine, and capers and roasted to a succulent golden brown. This flavorful entree is served with perfectly cooked fresh green beans and a very pretty yet simple long-grain and wild rice mixture flecked with bits of red, green, and yellow peppers. The menu has a number of other chicken entrees including free-range chicken roasted simply with rosemary, and cilantro chicken with avocado salsa. Silvercreek also has a number of fish and seafood entrees, including sauteed salmon, pecan catfish, and mahi-mahi teriyaki. Rounding out the menu are steak entrees, interesting salads, and sandwiches. Silvercreek's desserts are baked on the premises; the apple walnut pie a la mode makes a satisfying choice and is large enough for two. The spicy filling is full of chunky apples and topped with a crumbly walnut topping. Other dessert specials change daily. Silvercreek has a small but adequate wine list and many imported beers.

Timpone's
710 S. Goodwin Ave.
Urbana
(217) 344-7619
Open: Monday through Saturday
11:00 a.m.-10:00 p.m. (Saturday until 11:00 p.m.)
Price range: Moderate to expensive

A very popular spot for University of Illinois staff and Krannert Hall concert-goers, Timpone's is noted for its creative and sophisticated menu. The dishes at this restaurant have dual origins in Italian and California cuisine and feature the liberal use of fresh vegetables, herbs, fruits, and nuts in eclectic combinations. Typical of Chef Raymond Timpone's style might be such pairings as spinach with grilled pears and blue cheese; warm goat cheese with arugula; chicken with walnuts or pine nuts; venison with blackberries; and rabbit with fresh sorrel. Paté lovers will find the house paté served appropriately with good French bread, cornichons, nicoise olives, and mustard. For lunch Timpone's has homemade pasta specialties, excellent salads, and some unusual sandwiches. The ever-changing seasonal dinner menu always lists a fresh fish of the day, fresh homemade pasta selections, and an assortment of creatively prepared meat and poultry entrees; often you will find game meats, such as venison or pheasant, featured.

The pasta dishes here offer intriguing twists on traditional favorites or totally original combinations of ingredients. In a rich variation on traditional pasta with pesto sauce, cannelloni are stuffed with ricotta, spinach, and pine nuts, baked with mushrooms and mozzarella cheese, and served with a cream-softened version of rich pesto sauce. Other possibilities might be fettuccini Alfredo with fresh lemon; saffron linguine with mixed seafood and tomato; or spinach tagliatelle with chicken, mushrooms, cream, and pine nuts. Meat entrees are beautifully presented. Perfectly cooked double-cut lamb chops are dipped in a piquant sauce of Dijon mustard and chopped mint, rolled in breadcrumbs, grilled, and served with a color-coordinated array of four (red, yellow, green, and orange) fresh vegetables.

An interesting and hearty entree is grilled duck sausage with lentils, polenta, potatoes, and vegetables. Fish possibilities might be grilled jumbo scallops with tomato-basil sauce or grilled mahi-mahi with green peppercorn butter.

Desserts at Timpone's are very special. Only in Italy can you expect to find gelato this good, but in Italy the portion is one-third the size it is at Timpone's! And if that's not enough, the caramel sauce served with the gelato is exquisitely rich and creamy. The lemon tart has an intense and wonderfully flavored lemon-curd filling and is served with sweet chantilly. Other dessert possibilities might be the very rich chocolate decadence cake with tart-sweet raspberry sauce, macadamia nut tart with caramel ice cream, and creme caramel. Timpone's has a small but well-thought-out wine list that is heavy on California wines.

Vriner's
55 Main St.
Champaign
(217) 359-8973
Open: Daily
6:30 a.m.-8:00 p.m. weekdays (Monday until 4:00 p.m.)
Saturday 7:00 a.m.-12:30 p.m., Sunday 9:00 a.m.-2:30 p.m.
Price range: Inexpensive

Like many downtown areas, Champaign has a vacant look as many of its businesses have closed shop or moved out to mall locations. But some places continue to hang on or, in the case of Vriner's, to get a new lease on life. This nostalgic storefront restaurant with its pressed tin ceiling, beautiful wood and leaded-glass soda fountain, penny-candy counter, and wooden booths serves creative, vegetable-laden breakfasts, lunches, and dinners, as well as delicious ice-cream treats. For breakfast you can have eggs with hash browns or biscuits and gravy, and your choice of meat; French toast; buttermilk pancakes; fresh fruit and cheese crepes; an omelet; or a Tex-Mex selection. Breakfast entrees are served with fresh fruit and homemade muffins.

For lunch and dinner, Vriner's eclectic menu offers fresh, nicely prepared soups, salads, sandwiches, burgers, and entrees with an international flair. The grilled Greek chicken is marinated in a herb vinaigrette and grilled; it is moist, fresh, and flavorful and comes as a sandwich on freshly baked French bread with lettuce and tomato and sour cream-cucumber sauce, or as an entree with fried rice. Vriner's Greek salad is an unusual mixture of leafy lettuces, red onions, zucchini, green pepper, tomato, pepperoncini, and crumbled feta cheese in a very good vinaigrette. Other interesting possibilities include veggie casserole, eggplant sandwich on French bread, cilantro pesto pasta, Indonesian chicken with peanut butter sauce, and teriyaki rib eye stir-fry. The old-fashioned soda fountain is true to form with its old-fashioned treats: phosphates and egg creams, and floats, sodas, Bostons, and shakes that are made with delicious homemade ice-cream. During holiday season, Vriner's penny-candy counter has homemade candies such as candy canes at Christmas time, and peanut brittle, chocolates, and hard-candies from Thanksgiving through Valentine's Day.

Am-Ko Oriental Foods
32 Green St.
Champaign
(217) 398-2922
Open: Daily except Wednesday
10:00 a.m.-7:00 p.m. (open at noon on Thursday and until 6:00 p.m. on Sunday)

Am-Ko has shelves bulging with foods from such countries as Korea, Japan, India, Lebanon, Jordan, China, Thailand, and the Philippines. In its refrigerated cases there are a number of varieties of kimchee, Bulgarian cheese, Akawi cheese from Saudi Arabia, and Hallowini cheese from Cyprus. Packaged and canned foods including herbs, spices, rice fours, olive oil, noodles, flat breads, as well as cooking utensils and tea sets stock the shelves. It also has some fresh produce and frozen meat and fish.

Art Mart
127 Lincoln Square
Urbana
(217) 344-7979
Open: Daily
10:00 a.m.-9:00 p.m. (Monday through Friday)
10:00 a.m.-6:00 p.m. Saturday, Noon-5:00 p.m. Sunday

The Art Mart is central Illinois's largest and most complete kitchen, gourmet food, and gift shop. In addition to its selection of quality cookware, dinnerware, and flatware, it has the area's only large selection of imported cheeses, and imported and domestic deli meats and patés. It is here that you will locate hard-to-find tart pans, charlotte molds, heart-shaped angel-food cake tins, and gadgets galore. Gourmet specialty foods, flavored coffees, chocolates--including luscious Ruben's handmade Belgian chocolates (made in Danville)--are all here. This eclectic shop also has an excellent selection of children's toys and books, knitting yarns, and cookbooks. The baked goods are all made fresh on the premises daily--the delicious croissants are flaky and buttery and have lots of filling; the cookies are big and chewy, and the crusty French bread is the best in town. Out-of-town food lovers should not miss the opportunity to stop in at the Art Mart and stock up on their favorite delicacies.

Briney's Fresh Fish Market
406½ University
Champaign
(217) 351-5177
Open: Thursday, Friday, and Saturday
9:00 a.m.-6:00 p.m. (closes at 3:00 p.m. Saturday)

The sign in the window tells you what is available, but some of the most frequent offerings are fresh buffalo fish, perch, catfish, carp, frog legs, turtle, and shrimp. During morel mushroom season, mid-April through Mother's Day, watch the sign--morels are sometimes sold here.

Chang's Oriental Market
505 S. Neil
Champaign
(217) 356-9288
Open: Daily except Wednesday
10:00 a.m.-7:00 p.m. and 11:00 a.m.-6:00 p.m. Saturday

Chang's has a large selection of imported foods, similar to Am-Ko's; however, Chang's also has fresh noodles that can't be found anywhere else in town. You can also buy ingredients for Mexican dishes. Often you'll find unusual fresh seafood-- shrimp, softshell crab, or sea cucumbers, for example.

Great American Seafood Company
1711 W. Kirby
Champaign
(217) 352-0986
Open: Daily
10:00 a.m.-7:00 p.m. (12:00 p.m.-5:00 p.m. Sunday)

The Great American Seafood Company receives air shipments of fresh fish from all over the country and the world--Florida, Boston, Oregon, Utah, Alabama, Maine, Hawaii, and Norway. The fantastic selection of fresh seafood includes Dover sole, squid, Boston blue fish, mahi-mahi, Pacific red snapper, North Atlantic white fish, blue marlin, rainbow trout, Spanish mackerel, littleneck clams, cherrystone clams, mussels, herring, sea scallops, shrimp, Dungeness crab, oysters, and more. The homemade crab salad is delicious. The shop also has a selection of specialty foods and cookbooks.

Jarling's Custard Cup
309 W. Kirby
Champaign
(217) 352-2273
Open: Daily (March until end of November)
12:00 a.m.-10:00 p.m. (Sunday from 1:00 p.m.)

The season begins in early spring and lasts until around Thanksgiving at this popular frozen-custard shop. On a hot summer's evening it's hard to find a place to park and the line stretches out the door. This refreshing, surprisingly rich and soft "frozen custard" makes a delicious, light and low-calorie dessert. (It has 30% less butterfat and cholesterol than ice cream because it is ice milk.) One dip of any flavor, except chocolate, is 168 calories. It comes in vanilla, orange, lemon, chocolate, and strawberry; some flavors may not be available every day. You can order scoops of custard in a regular cone or waffle cone, and there is an extensive menu of "blizzard" options and sundaes and more.

Strawberry Fields Natural Food Market
306 W. Springfield
Urbana
(217) 328-1655
Open: Daily
8:00 a.m.-8:00 p.m. (Sunday 10:00 a.m.-6:00 p.m.)

Strawberry Fields is a full-service food market. It has all of the foods you'd expect to find in a natural food store as well as a whole wall of fresh, organic produce; a deli counter with take-out salads, sandwiches, and entrees; a frozen foods case with prepared foods; ice cream, and locally raised, organic, free-range chicken. Here you will also find a line of organic baby food and baby-care products, and an on-premises bakery. The bakery produces a variety of breads including buttermilk-oat rye, barley, sourdough, whole wheat, poppy seed, and herb breads. At the deli counter you can buy a slice of honey-wheat baklava, Linzer Torte, or cheesecake, and cookies that are chock-full of crunchy and chewy things. Strawberry Fields carries Laesch dairy products such as milk, buttermilk, and cream, some of which come in almost obsolete glass jars.

Sweet Indulgence
1701 W. Kirby
Champaign
(217) 352-2433
Open: Monday through Saturday
7:00 a.m.-7:00 p.m. (Saturday until 5:00 p.m.)

Sweet Indulgence has some wonderful baked goods. Particularly delicious are the European-style pastries, like the apple strip made with almond filling, sliced apples, and almonds on rich, flaky pastry or the moist and melt-in-your-mouth raspberry-almond tart. Scones and muffins are flavorful and have the right textures, but the croissants are too heavy. Each day the bakery has an assortment of majestic four-layer cakes in such flavors as Sachertorte, lemon torte, German chocolate, praline dacquoise, coconut, chocolate mocha, and black forest. Fresh French bread, Italian sourdough, buttermilk white, and honey-cracked wheat breads are available every day. The Italian sourdough, a hearty, round peasant bread with a wonderful coarse texture and chewy crust, is a very good choice. Sweet Indulgence has fruit pies, cream pies, brownies in four varieties, tea cookies, and much more available every day, as well as special-order items that need to be ordered a few days in advance.

Walnut Street Tea Company
115 S. Walnut
Champaign
(217) 351-6975
Open: Monday through Saturday
10:00 a.m.-6:00 p.m. (Saturday 11:00 a.m.-4:00 p.m.)

This striking beige tile shop has a large selection of teas, as well as flavored coffees, tea pots, and accessories. It also offers specialty food items such as honey, imported chocolates, cookies, candies, and juices. Teas, coffees, and herbs and spices are available in bulk. This shop depends on the vacuum packaging of its supplier for fresh coffee beans, and it was a pleasant surprise to find that the coffee was, indeed, fresh. You may buy the beans or have them ground.

Dalton City

Stoney's
120 Main St.
(217) 874-2213
Open: Every day
5:00 p.m.-9:00 p.m. (Friday and Saturday until 10:00 p.m. and Sunday from 4:00 p.m.)
Price range: Inexpensive to moderately expensive

Stoney's is 15 minutes southeast of Decatur, in Dalton City. When you enter the restaurant, you might notice the photos of cattle bedecked with blue ribbons. Keep walking-- unless you prefer to become acquainted with your dinner--and you will enter a lovely restaurant that looks like a tastefully decorated large home. Pegged wooden floors, wallpaper, and a brick fireplace combine to make this a warm and inviting place to enjoy a delicious meal. The 14-page menu at Stoney's not only lists the food and drinks available but gives patrons a chance to learn about various cuts of beef, about wine and food combinations, and a little about the owner's philosophy of life. The menu is loaded with salad, seafood, chicken, and pork selections, but the beef is so outstanding it is hard to imagine anyone but a strict vegetarian passing it by.

Dinners include soup, salad, and an entree with potato, noodles, or rice. The onion soup is served in a large crock and has croutons and melted cheese in a good parsley flavored beef broth. German potato soup with its unusual spices is also good. The salad here is typical of how Stoney's goes the extra mile to present something special: rather than serving a simple lettuce and tomato salad, this one has leafy lettuce, spinach, red cabbage, radishes, carrots, cucumber, and a cherry tomato (in season only) nicely arranged on the plate. It is served with a lazy Susan of four dressings. The French and thousand island dressings are fine, but the sweet, creamy poppy seed dressing with a hint of mustard is very good, as is the thick garlicky ranch dressing.

The prime rib is available in three sizes: petite cut, medium cut, and Diamond Jim cut. Served with hot broth and horseradish or a milder horseradish sauce, the meat is melt-in-your-mouth delicious. The beef blackstone is another excellent beef entree; two filets sauteed in butter are set on crisp croutons and topped with a rich sauce spiked with Madeira wine and fresh mushroom caps.

The dessert menu consists of six ice cream or fruit selections, or you can select something from a sweet tray, which is brought to the table. The strawberries sabayon is a very good choice from the menu, particularly during local strawberry season. The strawberries are served with a white-wine vanilla sauce and topped with real whipped cream. The Dutch apple pie from the sweet tray, which has a good filling and topping, unfortunately has a soggy crust.

Stoney's offers a large selection of imported beer, an unusual wine list, and a slew of cocktail creations for before and after dinner. This is a great place for a family meal (there are seven items on the child's menu), a night out with friends, or a special event.

Decatur

Mr. G's
701 E. Eldorado
(217) 423-1765
Open: Monday through Saturday
11:00 a.m.-6:00 p.m. (until 8:00 p.m. Monday through Friday in summer)
Price range: Inexpensive

At Mr. G's small hotdog stand you can sit at a counter or take out a great kosher-style hotdog. The hotdogs here are great for three reasons: they are all-beef Vienna hotdogs (from Chicago); they are not overcooked (a common problem for the less-experienced hotdog vendor); and they are served in the right kind of bun with the right kind of fresh condiments. Served in a poppy seed bun, the hotdog is dressed with your choice of mustard, sweet relish, onions, tomatoes, kosher pickles, sport peppers, and sauerkraut. French fries are optional, but don't miss them. The fresh, thin-cut fries are cooked until they are crisp and golden. Mr. G's also serves Italian beef, Italian sausage, Italian meatball sandwiches, chili, taco salads, and more.

Nick's
480 Brush College Rd.
(217) 422-2255
Open: Monday through Saturday
11:00 a.m.-9:00 p.m. (until 7:00 p.m. in winter and until 10:00 p.m. Friday and Saturday)
Price range: Inexpensive

Nick's is a family-run and family-oriented restaurant serving good Greek food. It is pleasantly decorated with white stucco walls and Greek decorations, and it has an outdoor patio set in a wooded area. The menu features a nice selection of

Greek appetizers including *saganaki* (flaming cheese), *spanakopita* (spinach pie), and *tyropita* (feta cheese pie), and four salads, including a Greek salad and a middle-eastern tabbullah salad made with cracked wheat, parsley, lemon juice and olive oil. Gyros or lamb kebab sandwiches on pita bread are available, as are American-style submarine sandwiches. Each day, two Greek specialties supplement the menu's four entrees: shish kebab, trout, spanakopita, and shish kebab combination.

The spanakopita, an individual pastry made with feta cheese, spinach, and onions wrapped in phyllo dough, has a tangy cheese flavor and a flaky, buttery crust. Hearty lamb stew has tender chunks of lamb simmered with tomatoes, onions, celery, zucchini, eggplant (or other seasonal vegetables) and is delicately spiced with herbs, lemon, and cinnamon. A large portion of stew is served on a bed of fluffy rice and is accompanied (on request) by a dish of fresh yogurt with crushed cucumber, green onions, and dill that nicely complements the stew. A lamb or similar Grecian stew is available Monday through Thursday. Look for chicken kebabs on Monday, *pastitsio* (macaroni, meat, and cheese-custard casserole) on Tuesday, spanakopita on Wednesday, Greek spaghetti on Thursday, *moussaka* (eggplant, meat, and cheese-custard casserole) and *dolma* (stuffed grape leaves) on Friday, and gyros and spanakopita on Saturday.

Nick's has a good selection of Greek pastries. Especially good are the *baklava* (phyllo dough layered with nuts and syrup and spiced with cinnamon), *kataif* (shredded dough with walnuts and syrup), and powered-sugar cookies. The menu has a few Greek wines as well as beer and liquor.

Tokyo Garden
2959 N. Oakland
(217) 875-1211
Open: Tuesday through Sunday
5:00 p.m.-9:00 p.m. (Friday and Saturday until 10:30 p.m.)
Price range: Moderate
Reservations advised

In the Teppan Room of this Japanese restaurant, fresh food is prepared right before your eyes at the grill built into your table. Not only will you have a delicious meal prepared in the centuries old *teppan*-style, but if your chef is in the mood, you will also be treated to a spectacle of knife artistry.

Teppan dinners include soup, salad, a shrimp appetizer (with beef entrees only), an entree, vegetables, and rice. For the very hungry, there are a number of appetizers on the menu. A good choice are *gyoza*, steamed and then pan-fried dumplings served with a soy-vinegar-based sauce. The shrimp gyoza are very delicate, thin-skinned dumplings stuffed with a chopped shrimp and green onion mixture. Diners can choose between onion or miso soup. The miso soup is a tasty broth with bits of green onion; the onion soup is bland. The salad has a nice, unusual ginger dressing, but water at the bottom of the salad bowl detracts from the simple salad by diluting the dressing.

After the salad, a chef arrives at your table to grill the entrees and vegetables. Each person receives two dipping sauces served in individual shallow bowls. The sweet-and-sour sauce is for seafood, and a hot mustard sauce is for beef and chicken. Most of the dishes are prepared in bite-sized pieces; the chef serves each dish as it is done, finishing his service with vegetables. Tasty morsels of shrimp are a wonderful beginning. The sea scallops are an excellent choice: golden brown and crisp on the outside, tender and succulent on the inside, with a sprinkling of sesame seeds that add a nutty flavor. The chicken is tender and flavorful and the steak is cooked to your liking. A mound of mixed seasonal vegetables is grilled at the table; the combination of zucchini, onions, and mushrooms is fresh and good. You may eat your meal with wooden chop sticks or a fork. Hot tea is served with the meal.

Dessert at Tokyo Garden is very low key. For a light, unusual choice try the green tea ice cream, a creamy, not overly sweet concoction with a subtle tea flavor and pretty green color.

Walker's Cafe
Corner of Locust and 22nd
(217) 422-8872
Daily
6:00 a.m.-3:00 p.m. (Saturday until 1:00 p.m., Sunday from
7:00 a.m.-1:00 p.m.)
Price range: Inexpensive

The hardworking people from the Staley, Caterpillar, and Firestone factories keep the coffeepots perking at this small cafe that serves "from scratch" hearty, home-style breakfasts and lunches. The breakfast menu includes biscuits and gravy, pancakes, eggs and meat, omelettes, and French toast, as well as the standard hot and cold cereals. For lunch, in addition to hamburgers, hot dogs, BLTs, and club sandwiches, there are daily hot specials such as nicely spiced hot meatloaf that comes sandwiched between white bread and served with mashed potatoes and brown gravy; macaroni and cheese; chicken fried steak; walleye; or ham and beans. Some of these specials are served with such side dishes as hominy, green beans, spinach, cauliflower, or broccoli. For dessert, there are usually three cream pies and one cake from which to choose.

Pete's Eats
118 N. Merchant
(217) 423-3287
Open: Monday through Saturday
9:00 a.m.-3:00 p.m. (Saturday until noon)

This small downtown deli carries the excellent Vie de France line of bakery products, including traditional crusty baguettes; multigrain baguettes made from whole wheat, rye, sunflower seeds, and molasses; croissants, both plain and filled; cookies; cinnamon rolls; and muffins. Everything is baked fresh daily.

Havana

Waterworth's Restaurant and Lounge
124 N. Plum
(309) 543-9156
Open: Monday through Saturday
11:00 a.m.-10:00 p.m. (Monday closed between 2:00 p.m.-4:00 p.m. and Saturday open at noon)
Price Range: Inexpensive

Although Waterworth's is a darkly lit bar, it is also a family restaurant with an old jukebox featuring 50s and 60s music. It has a large menu featuring appetizers, soups, salads, sandwiches, and dinners of steak, chicken, or fish, as well as a "kid's corner" of the menu. A special treat on this menu, which offers a number of nicely deep-fried items, is the breaded pork tender, made on the premises. It is crispy-crunchy on the outside, and meaty on the inside. This huge tenderloin is ridiculously perched on a regular sized hamburger bun. The restaurant has hearty daily lunch specials.

Waterworth's sometimes has morel mushrooms available in season. For more information see *Shopping for Morels*.

Vic's Specialty Shop
117 S. Plum
(309) 543-2240
Open: Monday through Saturday
6:30 a.m.-4:30 p.m. (Saturday until 2:00 p.m.)
Price Range: Inexpensive

Vic's is a small restaurant that serves inexpensive hearty breakfast and lunch, but what makes this little place special is its inexpensive bakery. Especially good are the "tea-time tassies," delectable pecan tartlets with a flaky crust and a sweet-crunchy filling; the zucchini bars, which are light and spicy; the small cinnamon rolls made with biscuit dough; and the large, gooey cinnamon rolls made with sweet dough. Vic's has croissants, assorted donuts, pies, turnovers, brownies, and more.

Jacksonville

The Terrace Tea Room
611 E. State St.
(217) 243-1319
Open: Monday through Saturday
9:00 a.m.-2:00 p.m.
Price range: Inexpensive

The Terrace Tea Room, located among the open shops of the renovated train depot, is one of a a half dozen or so tea rooms scattered throughout central Illinois. Although the Terrace Tea Room is a bit more bustling than most, it serves comfort food in a relaxed garden-like setting. Between 9:00 and 11:00 a.m., freshly baked cinnamon rolls and coffee are served, and lunch begins at 11:00 a.m. Although the menu is small, it is supplemented by daily specials. The Terrace salad comes in two sizes; the small one is quite adequate. Made with romaine lettuce, red pepper, real bacon bits, homemade croutons, grated cheese, and an excellent, creamy house dressing, this salad is a good choice for a light lunch. The cream of mushroom soup is rich and full of fresh mushrooms. The tortellini soup, a spicy chicken broth with shreds of chicken and meat-filled tortellini is also tasty. A nice entree is hot shrimp--tiny shrimp are abundant in a very rich and creamy sherry-flavored sauce; chopped hard-boiled eggs and pieces of mushrooms enrich this dish. Entrees are served with lettuce salad, cranberry salad, and a slice of wonderfully tangy and moist homemade lemon bread. Other possibilities are chicken salad, various sandwiches, and house specials such as chicken ala king, ham and broccoli in puff pastry, and Greek meat rolls.

Desserts, as well as breads, are all freshly baked. The rum cake is a very moist, lightly rum-flavored yellow bundt cake with a rich pecan struesel topping. The turtle crepe, a frozen, filled crepe with chocolate sauce, pecans, and whipped cream has a good flavor despite its slightly soggy crepe. Iced tea is fresh and abundant.

Jacksonville Transfer Company
611 E. State St.
(217) 243-1319
Monday through Saturday
9:00 a.m.-5:00 p.m.

The Jacksonville Transfer Company is a nice gift shop with a selection of gourmet cookware and specialty foods. Chocolates, teas, coffees, jellies, mustards, and spices are some of the items you will find. Look for a special bakery rack featuring some of the baked goods served at the Terrace Tea Room.

Kampsville

Louie's Kampsville Inn
River Mile 32 (at the Kampsville Ferry)
(618) 653-4413
Open: Daily
7:00 a.m.-1:00 a.m.
Price range: Inexpensive

Although this restaurant, just west of the Illinois River, is outside the geographic area of this book, it is such a part of river life that it is too interesting to ignore. A hotel and restaurant have been in this spot, serving the people that work the river, since 1880. When in this dark restaurant and lounge, you never forget that you are on the river: from the windows you can watch the river and the ferry. On the walls are photos of boats that have plied the river as well as watermarks depicting the water level of various floods. The menu has lots of local fish and other seafood. Louie's serves basic breakfast food, but it is known for its fresh catfish, served at lunch and dinner. A catfish fritter sandwich is a large portion of crisply fried strips of catfish served with two slices of white bread and two sauces--tartar and chili. Also on the menu are buffalo fish ("boned" fish), frog legs, shrimp, scallops, and fried chicken, steaks, hamburgers, ham steak, and more. Specialties include Cajun catfish, Cajun chicken, grilled catfish fillet, and hot chicken wings. Dinners are served with a choice of two side-dishes. The homemade Dutch apple pie, with its flaky crust, good apple filling, and crumbly topping, was a special treat.

Morel mushrooms are sometimes available here during morel season. See *Shopping for Morels* and call ahead for availability and to reserve them.

Lincoln

The Blue Dog Inn
111 S. Sangamon
(217) 735-9924
Price range: Inexpensive

The sign above the Blue Dog Inn says it all: "A civilized drinking establishment." This very attractive tavern has a tin ceiling, wainscotting, wooden booths and tables, and ceiling fans, which do a commendable job of keeping cigarette smoke under control. The tavern has a full menu including appetizers, salads, soups, "chilli," deli sandwiches, and dessert specials.

The house burger, a big, one-third pound burger served on black bread with Swiss cheese and grilled onions, is a hearty choice. The grilled mild red onions are soft and sweet, while the bread, also cooked on the grill, is nice and crunchy. Be sure to specify how you like your meat cooked, otherwise it might be slightly overcooked for some tastes. The crispy fries that come with the burger are cut thin and cooked with the skins on. Freshly brewed iced tea is an added bonus.

Guzzardo's Italian Villa
Arcade Building (rear) 509½ Pulaski
(217) 732-6370
Open: Tuesday through Saturday (longer pizza delivery hours)
4:30 p.m. to 10:00 p.m. (11:30 p.m. Friday and Saturday)
Price range: Inexpensive to moderate

Off the arcade of the Arcade Building is a small courtyard with a nice flower garden. At the end of the courtyard is Guzzardo's, a family-oriented restaurant that has been in business for more than 30 years. This is a good place to go before a movie for a quick hearty Italian meal or after a movie for pizza. It is not a place to linger over a romantic dinner--it has no wine and little atmosphere.

Guzzardo's features the usual assortment of Italian entrees and pasta specialties. Dinner starts at the salad bar, where you can build a salad from a variety of fresh vegetables and condiments including pepperoni, black olives, croutons, and cheddar cheese. There is a choice of six salad dressings. Standards like cottage cheese, apple sauce, potato salad, and coleslaw slaw are available. Also included with the salad bar are warm white and cracked wheat breads and a soup of the day. The large loaves of slice-your-own bread are hearty and good but the onion soup is bland.

The veal parmesan is made with real veal slices--not chopped, breaded veal patties. It comes with a nice zesty sauce that is full of green peppers, onions, and chunks of tomato. Served piping hot, the veal parmesan is topped with melted mozzarella cheese. The side order of spaghetti that comes with the veal has a simple sauce flavored with lots of basil. The manicotti is also a good selection. One tube holds a smooth and creamy cheese filling, and the other has a meat filling; the dish is topped with the same chunky sauce and mozzarella as on the veal parmesan. The dinner comes with warm garlic bread.

Guzzardo's also has good pizza made with homemade crust. The pizza is topped with lots of real mozzarella cheese and a nicely spiced sauce. There is a children's menu, with offerings such as a good sized hamburger served with a plate full of waffle-cut fries. Guzzardo's does not serve alcohol. It also does not serve dessert.

The Maple Club Dinner Theatre
Route 121 E.
(217) 735-1275
Dinner with live theater only
Reservations essential
Open: Call for schedule of productions

Food usually takes second billing to the dramatic performance at dinner theaters, but not so at the Maple Club. This small dinner theater produces excellent live theater. If possible, it matches the theme of its dinner selection to the particular production. For example, the menu for Pump Boys and Dinettes, a delightfully rollicking musical set in a gas station and diner, consisted of such diner favorites as "Salad greens, Granny's ol' fashion recipe of roast beef with smashed taters, pan gravy and sugar snap peas from the garden patch" or "Grandad's southern baked catfish." In fact, the "salad greens" had romaine lettuce, red cabbage, and homemade croutons, and an unusual choice of dressings including a tangy raspberry tarragon vinaigrette. This is hardly typical diner fare, but it is a fun way to be creative with the menu and the food. The theater itself is a good size so that everyone can see the stage, and although the tables are close together, your focus is on the stage not the next table's conversation. Your only choices in the meal are between two entrees and two desserts; the rest of the menu is not optional. So, if you're looking for a large menu selection, this is not your place. But, if you're looking for an evening of great entertainment and creative cooking, the Maple Club is a great choice.

Vintage Fare
414 Pulaski St.
(217) 732-5737
Open: Monday through Friday
10 a.m.-2:00 p.m.
Price range: Inexpensive

This lovely storefront restaurant with its lace curtains and restored ceiling and wall tiles is owned by the same people who own the Maple Club, Lincoln's well-respected live theater dinner club (reviewed in this section). The fresh, creative food at Vintage Fare is homemade and changes to take advantage of the season's freshest fruits and vegetables. There are always salads, sandwiches, soups, a hot entree of the day, and home-baked desserts. You walk up to a deli counter where you choose the items for your salad or sandwich. A typical salad special of the day: marinated broccoli salad made with crisply cooked broccoli and cauliflower with celery and carrots in a light tarragon-flavored vinaigrette is fresh and delightful.

Chicken salad, seafood salad, and tuna salad are available daily. The chicken salad is fresh and creamy and seafood salad is a delicate combination of crab meat, celery, fresh parsley, and a touch of onion. Sandwiches are served on your choice of freshly baked French roll, crescent roll, or stone-ground wheat roll. The crusty French roll is fresh and light. Other sandwich possibilities are freshly baked breast of turkey, roast beef, and baked ham. American, Swiss, or cheddar cheese can be added. The coffee served at Vintage Faire is freshly ground and a daily selection of homemade brownies, cookies, pies, and cakes make tempting desserts.

Beans & Such
202 S. Chicago
(217) 735-5520
Open: Tuesday through Saturday
10:00 a.m.-5:00 p.m. (Saturday 9:00 a.m.-4:00 p.m.)

Beans and Such is an elegant shop located next door to the Corner Cakery. It offers a large variety of flavored coffees, plus an assortment of teas, pastas, jams, sugarless fruit spreads, nuts, dried fruit, and other specialty food items. It also carries a selection of teapots, cups, and cooking accessories.

The Corner Cakery
200 S. Chicago
(217) 735-3829
Open: Monday through Saturday
7:00 a.m.-5:00 p.m. (4:00 p.m. Saturday)
Price range: Inexpensive

The Corner Cakery is a charming little bakery specializing in delicious, fresh-baked goods. Whole wheat bread, raisin bread, and French or Italian bread are available daily. Raisins alone flavor the dough of the Corner Cakery's unusual and hearty raisin bread. Whole wheat buns are made from the same dough as the whole wheat bread; both are moist, chewy, and flavorful. Buttery, flaky croissants, baked daily, come plain or filled with such tempting fillings as chocolate, strawberry and cheese, blueberry and cheese or strawberry jam. Moist and flavorful muffins have seasonal ingredients, so you might find orange-cranberry, date-nut, or blueberry, featured at different times of the year.

The Corner Cakery bakes two kinds of delicious fruit pies each day. Blackberry pie is loaded with fruit that is slightly tart; the filling has a very good consistency; and while the pastry is not especially tender, it is sweet and substantial--like a cobbler crust. The large chocolate chip cookies are good and the decorated cookies are beautiful. The Corner Cakery also bakes decorated cakes for special order.

Litchfield

Ariston Cafe
Old Route 66 (Off I-55 exit 52)
(217) 324-2023
Open: Daily
11:00 a.m.-11:00 p.m. (10:00 a.m.-10:00 p.m. Sunday)
Price range: Inexpensive to moderate

Litchfield is halfway between Springfield and St. Louis on I-55. With its well-advertised fast-food restaurants and gas stations it is a common place to stop. Many times after flying in to St. Louis to drive the rest of the way home from a family vacation, we've stopped at one of those chain restaurants. Never again, now that we've discovered the Ariston Cafe. This excellent family restaurant has been in Litchfield since 1924 and in its present building since 1935. Once inside the unimposing brick building you are taken back in time by the well-preserved wooden countertop and wooden booths, and wooden tables set for dinner with white tablecloths and fresh flowers. Fortunately, the menu is not of the past. It combines such classic favorites as prime rib, steak, and spaghetti, with updated items such as enchiladas, grilled chicken salad, and toasted ravioli appetizer.

Dinner begins with a visit to the soup and salad bar, which along with a choice of vegetable or potato, is included with dinner. The soup selections vary daily. The vegetable soup is good and the cream of mushroom soup is thick, rich, and full of mushrooms. In addition to the usual makings of tossed salad, this salad bar has some wonderful and unusual prepared salads: marinated broccoli salad, baby carrot salad, garlicky bean salad, and a sauerkraut salad in a sweet dressing with red pepper pieces.

The deep-fried meat ravioli is sprinkled with parmesan cheese and served with a dish of "spaghetti" meat sauce. The sauce is thick and hearty, but the ravioli dough becomes tough and dry when fried, which is too bad since it detracts from their very good meat filling.

The prime rib, cut one-inch thick, is melt-in-your-mouth tender and comes with American fries are cooked, sliced, and then fried on the grill until crisp. The deep-fried catfish come two to the order and are fresh and very good.

A dessert tray is brought to the table with plenty to tempt you. There is a choice of 10 desserts including chocolate or lemon delight cheesecake, bread pudding with rum sauce, baklava, apple dumpling, snicker pie, chocolate suicide cake, and carrot cake. The chocolate suicide cake was disappointing-- too dry and dense. Chocolate lovers are better off trying the snicker pie which has good, gooey caramel, peanuts, chocolate, and a cream cheese layer on a flaky crust. Another good dessert is the homemade baklava, the Greek, syrup soaked nut strudel, which was moist inside, flaky outside, and spicy.

Meredosia

The Approach Inn
North side of Main St.
(217) 584-1834
Open: Daily
6:30 a.m.-10:00 p.m.
Price Range: Inexpensive

The Approach Inn is a place where hardworking people can go for breakfast before work, a hot lunch, or a steak or catfish dinner and drink after work. This dark tavern at the foot of the bridge spanning the Illinois River is filled with round oak tables with huge clawfeet and wooden booths. A blackboard lists the day's specials and a large menu features catfish and steaks. The catfish is good, and the hot lunch specials are stick-to-your-ribs kinds of meals.

The Approach Inn sells morel mushrooms during season. For more information see *Shopping for Morels*.

Monticello

AnnaLee's Tea Room
223 E. Livingston
(217) 762-5456
Open: Monday through Friday
11:00 a.m.-3:00 p.m.
Price range: Inexpensive

AnnaLee's Tea Room provides a different lunching experience from the bustling atmosphere at the Brown Bag (reviewed next). Located inside the Leiper Furniture Store and decorated in Victorian-style with lace, flowered wallpaper, and antiques, the restaurant serves comfort food in a pampered atmosphere.

Lunch Bon Vivant consists of a hot entree of the day, a choice of soup or salad, and a basket of homemade breads. The salad of lettuce, shredded carrots and cheddar cheese, has a few Chinese noodles sprinkled on top. The house ranch dressing has a hint of bacon which mixes nicely with the noodles. The hot entree of the day, "My Ladies Pocket," is a flaky puff pastry filled with a chicken, rice, and vegetable mixture and topped with a cream sauce. It is unusual and flavorful. The rye and white breads served with the lunch are not special, but the pumpkin bread with raisins is very moist and good.

AnnaLee's menu has 13 teas from which to choose. Served in an individual tea pot, the tea is made correctly by steeping loose tea (contained in a tea dispenser) in hot water. The blackberry rum tea was fragrant and flavorful.

After lunch, a tray of desserts is brought to the table. You may be able to choose from a cream pie, a brownie sundae, a fruit pie, or a cheesecake. The marble cheesecake is served with chocolate sauce and whipped cream and is creamy and good.

The Brown Bag Deli-Restaurant and Pies by Inge
204-212 W. Washington
(217) 762-9221
Open: Monday through Saturday
9:00 a.m.-7:00 p.m. (Saturday until 5:00 p.m.)
Pies available Tuesday through Saturday after 11:00 a.m.
Price range: Inexpensive

California native Arlene Swing has created a wonderful deli with a large innovative menu by using fresh ingredients and refusing to take shortcuts. That means the cheese on your burrito is freshly grated on the premises rather than purchased already grated, and the turkey in your sandwich is roasted at the restaurant rather than bought precooked.

You place your order at a counter and then help yourself to dill pickles and pepperoncini. There is always a salad and soup of the day (except when the weather is too hot for soup). Creamy-cheesy broccoli soup is especially popular. The Scandinavian salad is a slawlike salad with raw broccoli, cauliflower, green pepper, carrots, cabbage, green onion, grated cheese, bacon, and sunflower seeds in a sweet dressing.

The sandwiches are loaded with fresh, moist meats and cheeses and are served on your choice of challah (egg bread), dark rye, wheat, onion roll, kaiser roll, or pita bread. The challah, which comes from Chicago, is a special treat; it is moist and chewy, just as it should be. Other sandwiches are made on bagels or croissants.

The deli has an old-fashioned soda fountain, which serves delicious real lemonade, phosphates, sodas, and other ice cream concoctions. The homemade ice cream has a 12% butterfat content.

Inside the deli is one counter devoted to pies and other baked goods made by Inge. These pies are really special. The crust, made partly with whole wheat flour, is tender and flaky. The apple pie has a flavorful apple filling and a crispy struesel topping with lots of spices. Her wonderful raspberry-blackberry pie is loaded with real fruit and the moist blueberry muffin has pecans in a struesel topping. Chocolate lovers should try the brownies--they are thick and gooey and full of nuts, caramel, and marshmallows.

The Brown Bag also has a small gourmet shop where you can buy many of the items used in the deli's recipes. This is a restaurant that is sure to have something for everyone.

Naples

Riverboat Trading Company
Mile 66 Illinois River
(217) 754-3457
Open: Wednesday through Sunday
5:00 p.m.-8:00 p.m. (until 9:00 p.m. in summer and Sunday
from 11:00 a.m.-8:00 p.m.)
Price Range: Inexpensive

The Riverboat Trading Company is the only reason--and a good one at that--to go to Naples. It is a lovingly decorated restaurant and bar that is housed in a restored brick mansion built in 1829. You can sit by one of the 10 fireplaces and gaze out at the river and imagine what Naples was like when it was a thriving river town. The menu is simple, with nicely prepared meals that take advantage of the location by serving catfish and buffalo fish, which although they might be pond-raised, certainly evoke a sense of locale.

The restaurant offers seven appetizers, including homemade onion rings, fried cheddar cheese nuggets, fried chicken livers, and spicy chicken wings. Seafood sandwiches at the Riverboat are large portions of crisply fried buffalo fish, catfish, or clams served with two slices of white bread, tartar sauce, and a slice of red onion. Buffalo fish is a mild, flaky white fish and as fresh as can be. It has a wonderfully crisp, corn-meal-based breading. Fish dinners come with a plain salad or cottage cheese, and a potato. The hash browns are a good choice. In addition to fish, the Riverboat offers fried chicken, steak, and shrimp scampi, a slightly garlicky dish of seven shrimp swimming in too much butter. Also available are hamburgers and beef tenderloin sandwiches. An inexpensive children's menu reinforces the welcome to children. Two types of good cheesecake end a simple but very pleasant meal. The restaurant is wheelchair accessible.

Oakland

Windowpanes Tea Room
3 Montgomery St.
(217) 346-2289
Open: Monday through Saturday
11:00 a.m.-2:00 p.m.
Price range: Inexpensive

Charming and cozy, the Windowpanes Tea Room is located in the Inn on the Square, the area's loveliest bed-and-breakfast. The menu features soups, salads, a quiche of the day, sandwiches made on croissants, and decadent desserts. One hot summer day, the soup special was a cold strawberry soup made with whipped strawberries, half-and-half, and sour cream. It was cool and refreshing. Available daily is a tasty version of French onion soup, made with beef stock flavored with sweet wine, onions, and topped with bread and toasted mozzarella cheese.

The seafood pasta salad is a good choice. Lots of crab meat and baby shrimp are mixed with shell pasta, celery, green onions, and a creamy dill dressing. The chef salad has fresh lettuce and spinach, ham, radishes, croutons, and sliced egg. The poppy seed dressing is fine but a little sweet. The salads are served with a wonderful flaky, buttery croissant, which is brought warm to the table. There is a small selection of desserts. Iced tea is fresh, clear, and plentiful. Although not on the menu, a peanut butter and jelly sandwich is available for children who do not find anything tempting on the menu.

Guests at the bed-and-breakfast can expect a hearty hot breakfast, which includes a delicious croissant.

Oakland Bakery
Main St. (on the square)
(217) 346-2322
Open: Tuesday through Saturday
5:00 a.m.-5:00 p.m (Saturday until 4:00 p.m.)

The Oakland Bakery has been in town for more than 70 years. It provides town residents with inexpensive freshly baked goods such as cookies, donuts, Danish pastries, rolls, breads, and noodles. Most of the items are uninspired, but some of the cookies were good--specifically the Mexican wafer, the cowboy (with oatmeal, coconut, pecans, and chocolate chips), and the elephant ear. Honey-wheat bread and raisin bread were both good and very inexpensive. The homemade noodles are a popular item.

Pana

Victorian House Tea Room and Gift Shop
311 S. Locust
(217) 562-5131
Open: Monday through Saturday
11:00 a.m.-2:00 p.m.
Price range: Inexpensive

This is one of a half dozen or so tea houses in central Illinois that invite you to have lunch or tea in a warm, homey setting. Many of the tea rooms double as gift shops and sell a few gift items and cookbooks. The Victorian House is unusual in that it has a gift shop on the second floor that is chock-full of unusual gifts and jewelry.

The Victorian House is just that--a large brick house with inlaid wood floors, oak tables, oriental-type rugs, a fireplace, decorative antiques, and a ceiling fan. The menu has only eight entrees, but has enough variety to satisfy everybody. The daily special, casserole lunch, includes a salad, two egg rolls, and a muffin. The chicken noodle broccoli casserole has thick chewy noodles, broccoli, and chicken, and while good, it is a bit bland. The eggrolls are delicious--pencil thin, tightly rolled, and filled with meat primarily, but some vegetables too, including crunchy water chestnuts. The date muffin is moist and sweetened with the distinctive flavor of dates. The iced tea was freshly brewed, and a pitcher with refills made the rounds frequently.

Not to be missed is the blackberry cobbler. Packed with blackberries, it was just the right consistency, and if the crust was a bit soggy from reheating, it was worth the trade-off to have it served warm and fragrant with berries.

Paris

L'Auberge
309 N. Main
(217) 463-2656
Open: Tuesday through Saturday
5:00 p.m.-9:00 p.m.
Price Range: Moderate to expensive

You might think you're in Paris, France, not Paris, Illinois, when you eat at L'Auberge. The food at this charming, converted Kentucky Fried Chicken is classic French and it is superb. Chef Daniel Sineau owned a restaurant in Paris, France, where he cooked for more than 20 years. He and his wife, Michele, decided to open a restaurant in Paris, Illinois, because they liked the town's name! Here, you can sample dishes from an amazingly large and varied menu, including a full page of first courses listing hot and cold appetizers, soups, and salads; entrees with classic sauces like bearnaise, hollandaise, or mornay; and pastries made with real buttercream. You can choose from a fixed-price menu and enjoy an appetizer, salad, entree with fresh vegetables, and a dessert for an incredibly low price. Or you can order from the a la carte menu. The menu at L'Auberge offers chicken, veal, steak, pheasant, quail, lasagna, seafood, and fish--all artfully prepared. It has a basic selection of French wines.

The hearty duck paté, made with duck, pork, and veal, is served with toast triangles. The French onion soup is made with a poultry stock sweetened with onions and wine and is topped with a crouton and cheese. An outstanding appetizer is *cuisses de grenouille Provencal* (frog legs Provencal). This buttery-rich dish consists of three pairs of frog legs sauteed with lots of garlic, fresh parsley, and tomatoes. For a light, cold appetizer try *les legumes ala Grecque* (marinated fresh mushrooms and artichoke bottoms); the fresh vegetables are tossed in a very light herbal vinaigrette. The dinner salad, which comes with the entree, is not special, but the house dressing is a piquant mustard dressing that is very interesting.

Petit tournedos de boeuf, an excellent selection from the fixed-price menu, consists of two large medallions of beef tenderloin on top of toast, topped with bordelaise sauce. The sauteed beef is tender and delicious and is served with the day's vegetables, in this case, perfectly cooked, diagonally sliced carrots and broccoli in hollandaise sauce, and delicious pan-fried potato wedges with herbs. Another selection from the fixed-price menu, *canard roti a l'orange*, a nicely prepared roast duck in a not-too-sweet orange sauce, is served with the same wonderful vegetables.

An outstanding dish from the a la carte menu is the *saumon en feuillete* (salmon in puff pastry). Brought to the table piping hot, this beautiful flaky cloud of pastry encrusting a fresh filet of salmon sits atop chopped mushrooms and shallots sauteed in butter. Fresh lemon slices on the salmon impart a fresh, tangy flavor to the fish, which is complemented by a rich hollandaise sauce. An excellent chef's special of the day (not on the menu) is lamb in mustard sauce. The lamb is melt-in-your-mouth tender, cooked medium rare, and served with a creamy and piquant mustard sauce with lots of garlic. The day's vegetables--sweet carrots, broccoli, and twice-baked potato with a velvety smooth potato filling artfully piped into the shell--accompany both main courses.

Dessert is not to be missed. There are four desserts on the menu in addition to an assortment of pastries that are brought to your table. The apple tart, a pastry filled with almond cream and topped with glazed sliced apples is superb. Another excellent choice is the cream puff. Really two cream puffs, a large one topped by a small one, both are filled with a creamy chocolate mousse and decorated with piped buttercream and a glaze of semisweet chocolate.

Petersburg

George Warburton's Food and Drink
R.R. 3, Box 191
(217) 632-7878
Open: Tuesday through Sunday
11:00 a.m.-9:00 p.m. (until 10:00 p.m. Friday and Saturday)

George Warburton's is a pretty restaurant that is only one mile north of New Salem State Park, so visitors to the park might want to stop in for lunch. The hamburger and freshly cut fries are good. This restaurant specializes in pork, and while the quality of the meat is good, some of the pork dinners are disappointing because of their bland sauces. If you choose unwisely, you can console yourself with dessert. Your server will bring a tray to the table with six or seven choices. The toffee cheesecake is creamy and has a good quality caramel topping. Other possibilities might be turtle pie made with a graham cracker crust, caramel, pecans, and chocolate chips; raspberry rhapsody, a raspberry and coconut cake; or chocolate chip cake with hot fudge sauce.

Pleasant Plains

La Casita
4th and Cartwright
(217) 626-1588
Open: Tuesday through Sunday
11:00 a.m.-2:00 p.m. and 5:00 p.m.-10:00 p.m.
(Saturday from 11:00 a.m.-10:00 p.m. and Sunday from 11:00
a.m.-4:00 p.m.)
Price range: Moderate
Reservations recommended for dinner

Visitors to New Salem will welcome the relaxed ambience of this charming Mexican and southwestern-style restaurant. The outdoor patio and southwestern art and knick-knack shop make it all the more attractive. Crispy fried flour tortilla chips and spicy salsa are served while you read the menu and make your meal selection. Here you'll find the usual Mexican specialties: tacos are served in hard corn tortillas; enchiladas are made with soft flour tortillas and have melted cheese and onion bits on top; and tasty tamales with lots of meat filling are served with thin bean chili. The a la carte refried beans and rice are good accompaniment. A taco salad is served in a flour tortilla shell with a side dish of tasty salsa. Other regular menu items are chimichangas, chile rellenos, tostados, chalupas, burritos, and for the timid, hamburgers and hot dogs. La Casita serves a variety of Mexican beer and a wide variety of specialty drinks, making this a very pleasant place to sit on the patio and relax on a warm summer night.

Pontiac

Buster's
603 S. Deerfield Rd.
(815) 844-7323
Open: Daily
6:00 a.m.-9:00 p.m. (until 10:00 p.m. Friday and Saturday)
Price range: Inexpensive

Halfway between Chicago and Springfield, serving full breakfasts, lunches, and dinners, Buster's is an alternative to fast-food chains for travelers who want to stop for a bite to eat and a place to stretch their legs. Dieters will be especially glad to know about this restaurant because it has a special "heart smart" menu that identifies calories, fat, sodium, and cholesterol levels in the selections on the special menu. Buster's has an all-you-can-eat buffet, that, unfortunately, suffers the fate of many such buffets: the food is dry. A better option is to select something from the menu. A good choice is the Buster melt, a juicy, charcoal-grilled burger served between two thick, toasted slices of freshly baked bread, and topped with sweet grilled onions and American and Swiss cheese. Another good item is the fried chicken breast sandwich. Served on a sesame seed bun, the moist chicken is fried in a light, homemade batter. Buster's is a good family restaurant.

Springfield

The Barrel Head
1577 Wabash
(217) 787-2102
Open: Daily
11:00 a.m.-1:00 a.m. (from noon Sunday)
Price range: Inexpensive

The Barrel Head is a short, squat-looking pub that is surprisingly bright inside. It has good hamburgers and fries and more than a dozen draft beers, including imported ones such as Harp Lager, Guinness Stout, Heineken, and Becks. Good quality, lean ground chuck or sirloin and grilling (not frying) make the burgers special. For a fancier burger try the patty melt. It has sharp cheddar cheese and grilled onions on a lean burger and is sandwiched between two pieces of grilled black rye. Or try the Chef's Pride, a seasoned, half-pound burger studded with cheddar cheese bits, wrapped in bacon, and served on a homebaked roll. The Barrel Head has a large menu with salads, sandwiches, horseshoes, chicken, and dinner specials. It also has a children's menu, but the place is a tavern, which sometimes gets smoky, so if the smoke bothers you or your children, ask to be seated in the beer garden, which is open when the weather is nice.

Boyd's Family Style Restaurant
1831 S. Grand Avenue E.
(217) 744-0248
Open: Tuesday through Saturday
7:00 a.m.-3:00 p.m. (until 8:00 p.m. Friday and noon Saturday)
Price range: Inexpensive

Boyd's is a great place for southern-style food. The problem is that the restaurant is only open one evening, so if you can't get there on Friday, you'll have to squeeze in dinner during lunch hour. But let's start with breakfast--it's taken seriously at Boyd's. Hearty eaters will love the Big Boyd's. It includes two eggs; a huge plate of good homemade biscuits smothered in creamy, Louisiana-style white sausage gravy nicely spiced with sage, rosemary, and thyme; delicious sliced potatoes fried with onions and green pepper; a bowl of smooth grits, and your choice of meat--all for a pittance! The sausage patties are mildly spiced with herbs and cooked until crisp on the outside. The buttermilk pancakes at Boyd's are light, tender, and moist. In addition to the many staple breakfast choices, the breakfast menu has some new items: a Creole omelette, a vegetable omelette, and a steak or pork chop breakfast.

Boyd's has daily dinner specials in addition to regular menu items. Catfish and buffalo fish are served fresh every Friday. Cajun chicken, originally a Friday special, is now a regular item. Not for tender tastebuds, this breaded chicken breast, served over rice and smothered in gravy spiced with an unusual blend of fiery Cajun spices, is a very good choice. It is served with fresh vegetables; the green beans are cooked with bits of bacon and onion. Boyd's cornbread, served warm, is tasty and moist. Another good choice is the gumbo, which is chock-full of chicken, ham, sausage, shrimp, okra, celery, onions, tomatoes, and herbs, and served in a big bowl over rice. For a special summer treat try the fried okra. These golden nuggets of fresh okra are fried in a cornmeal batter until crispy. Other items on the menu at Boyd's are hamburgers, horseshoes, fried chicken, liver and onions, and ribs.

Save room for dessert at Boyd's. The fillings in the sweet potato pie and the buttermilk pie are so good that you can ignore the mediocre crust. The sweet potato pie is smooth, light, and spiced with lots of nutmeg and clove. The buttermilk pie has a rich, creamy filling with a crunchy sugary top. Although there is no special children's menu, this restaurant has many inexpensive items and welcomes children.

Capital Downtown Cafe
312 E. Monroe St.
(217) 522-5162
Open: Tuesday through Saturday
5:00 p.m.-9:00 p.m. (until 10:00 p.m. Friday and Saturday)
Price range: Inexpensive

By night, the Capital Downtown Cafe sheds its hash-slinging persona and serves exotic Indian and Pakistani food. Some of the food at this simple storefront restaurant is as delicious as it is unique. A nice selection of appetizers will quickly introduce you to the distinctive flavors of this cuisine. The *shami kabob* is a grilled patty made from ground steak, garlic, lentils, peppers, and spices. It is unusually smooth, sneak-up-on-you spicy hot, and delicious. The *chapli kabob* has the texture of a hamburger patty, is differently spiced than the shami kabob, and is also very good. *Samosa* is a deep-fried triangle-shaped turnover. The dough is light and crispy, and the filling of ground beef, green onions, and spices is good. For a milder appetizer, try cutlets, which are grilled patties made from mashed potatoes, onions, green peppers, and spices. *Pakora*, another good, mild choice, is strips of vegetables such as green pepper, carrots, onions, potatoes, and zucchini that are dipped in a cumin-flavored batter and deep-fried. The appetizers are served with three sauces: a white, yogurt-based mild and slightly sweet sauce; a brown, tangy medium-hot sauce; and a red-hot sauce. Each sauce has unique combinations of spices and chilies, and they make good additions to the appetizers. Three types of fried bread are available. *Papadum* is a large deep-fried wafer with green chiles. Although tasty, it can be a bit too greasy. *Poorie* is a very flaky deep-fried flat bread, and *naan* is a grilled, flat yeast bread much like the familiar pita bread.

Capital Downtown Cafe has vegetable, chicken, beef, lamb, and shrimp entrees. An excellent choice is *tandori murqie,* one-half of a chicken that has been marinated in a paste made of numerous spices and chillies and then grilled. This tender and very spicy entree is served with rice and yogurt sauce. Another good choice is *kadhai goosht*, chunks of lamb stewed in a tomato-based sauce with onions, garlic, cinnamon, cloves, and other spices. *Kadhai murqie* is the chicken version of the same dish. Both are served with naan. *Biryani* dishes are large portions of rice with turmeric, cardamon, and other spices and either pieces of chicken, mixed vegetables, or beef that have been marinated. The best of these is the *sabzee biryani* (vegetable) because the vegetables more successfully absorb the spices in the marinade and also because they provide needed moistness to the rice. The beef in the goosht biryani is dry and unpleasant.

Your server will tell you about desserts. There are usually two or three Pakistani desserts in addition to cheesecake. A good Pakistani dessert is made with dried apricots and a dollop of creamy custard; it has a special sweet-tart flavor. The white chocolate cheesecake is creamy but not particularly special.

The Feed Store
516 E. Adams
(217) 528-3355
Open: Monday through Saturday
11:00 a.m.-3:00 p.m.
Price range: Inexpensive

Housed in a rehabilitated Lincoln-era building on the square across from the Old State Capitol, The Feed Store remains a popular lunch spot, serving fresh, hearty, creative deli-fare in a congenial atmosphere.

Homey and satisfying soups are the linchpin of this restaurant's popularity. You will not find leftover vegetables in Feed Store soup--only fresh vegetables are used, and the unusual-looking greens in your salad might be endive or escarole added to a mixture of the day's freshest lettuces. The Feed Store also uses only real dairy products so the calorie-or-cholesterol-conscious may want to avoid the cream soups, but the rest of us will enjoy the taste and texture that only real butter and cream provide. The Feed Store serves five or six different soups daily. The mushroom bisque, cream of spinach and mushroom, and beef barley are excellent choices. Some other interesting soup possibilities are cream of watercress, Wisconsin cheese, seafood chowder, and chicken and corn.

The menu at The Feed Store is large and varied, offering sandwiches of cold cuts, meat salads, and cheeses on your choice of seven types of bread. Also featured are six vegetarian selections including an interesting sandwich of pecans, olives, pimentos, and cream cheese on pumpernickel bread. The chicken salad, made with fresh chicken, celery, spices, and real mayonnaise, is creamy and satisfying. Meats are appealing-- turkey is moist breast meat, the beef is top round roasted medium rare, and the salami is German-style and aged until hard. For a lighter meal there are three salads with a choice of seven dressings. The Feed Store bakes its own wonderfully creamy cheesecakes, which come in four flavors.

The Foreigner's
220 S. 6th
(217) 522-1989
Open: Monday through Saturday
11:00 a.m.-3:00 p.m. (until 2:00 p.m. Saturday)

Greek food is the "foreign" fare at this cafeteria-style restaurant, which is open for lunch only. In addition to gyros, cheese-spinach pie, and Greek salads, the Foreigner's serves "old country" stick-to-your-ribs hot meals such as moussaka, stuffed cabbage rolls, a vegetable stew called *briam*, and lasagna. The gyros sandwich is made with thin-sliced gyros meat, a thick yogurt sauce, onions, and chopped tomatoes tucked into grilled pita bread. The meat could be crispier, but it is flavorful, and the sandwich is not greasy--a common fate of gyros sandwiches cooked by the inexperienced. The cheese-spinach pie has a very tasty filling of spinach, feta cheese, and onions, but the phyllo crust is slightly soggy.

A number of hot meals are noteworthy. The moussaka--a casserole of layered sliced potatoes and zucchini, ground meat, clove-and-herb-flavored tomato sauce, and creamy custard--has a very good and unusual flavor. The hearty cabbage rolls are filled with a rice, ground beef, and a herb mixture and served with a spicy tomato sauce. Briam, a vegetable stew made with potatoes, onions, zucchini, and tomatoes, in a tomato sauce with lots of fresh garlic, is another good choice. The lasagna, which has cottage cheese floating throughout the layers of pasta and meat sauce, is too salty. The Foreigner's has uninteresting baklava for dessert.

Magic Kitchen Thai Restaurant
4112 Peoria Rd.
(217) 525-2230
Open: Tuesday through Saturday
5:00 p.m.-10:00 p.m.
Price range: Inexpensive

Thai food is a cuisine of contrasts. Fiery peppers are paired with the cool refreshing flavors of cucumber, lemon, or lime. Chopped peanuts add crunch to slick noodles. And matchstick-cut bamboo shoots add texture to softly sauteed vegetables. These are some of the reasons that customers are willing to stand in the inevitable lines at this plain and noisy restaurant. Newcomers to Thai cuisine are wise to take heed of the menu's description: "Thai food is spicy. Mild is spicy to most people. Medium is hot. Hot is devastating." There are a number of vegetarian items on the menu.

Start your meal with egg rolls, which at the Magic Kitchen are tightly wrapped little rolls with finely chopped vegetables mixed with delicate Thai spices. Brought to the table crispy and hot from the deep fryer, they are served with a hot-peppery peanut sauce. Two soups are especially noteworthy. The lemon grass soup is a hot-peppery broth flavored with lemon grass and other Thai spices and made with your choice of beef, pork, chicken, shrimp, or fish. Perhaps even more interesting is Bume noodle soup, which is served "wet" with broth, or "dry" with peanuts and lime. If you order it dry with shrimp, a bowl of fresh shrimp, long curly noodles, bean sprouts, fried tofu, fried wontons, chopped cilantro, chopped peanuts, and fresh lime will arrive at your table to acquaint you with the unique flavors of Thailand.

Entrees at the Magic Kitchen are stir-fried dishes with lots of fresh vegetables, Thai spices, and usually a choice of meat, fish, or shrimp. Some are served over rice while some are served over rice noodles, transparent bean thread noodles, or fried wontons. Pad Thai is a meatless dish with pan-fried noodles, bean sprouts, egg, fried tofu, green onions, chopped peanuts, and lime. Although it can be a bit dry, it is a good tasty dish. The "basil" dishes are very good. Your choice of beef, pork, or chicken is stir-fried with fresh (when available) basil leaves, mushrooms, onions, and peppers. This is a peppery dish and will be prepared to your order--from mild to hot. The curry dishes, both red and green, are delicious, but deceptively hot. Another good and unusual dish is three-flavor fish, in which fresh chunks of fish are stir-fried with pineapple, vegetables, and ginger in a spicy, but not sweet, sauce. In addition to the twenty or so entrees listed on the menu, there are sometimes daily specials listed on the blackboard. Ask your server for advice if you are unsure of what to order.

Magic Kitchen regulars swear by the homemade pies that you'll find listed on the blackboard. If flaky crust isn't important to you, try a slice of fresh fruit pie or macadamia nut pie--at least the fillings are good.

Maldaner's
222 S. Sixth St.
(217) 522-4313

Maldaner's has been in downtown Springfield since 1884, but it wasn't until 1981, when Chef Michael Higgins arrived that it became a truly distinguished restaurant. Higgins, a product of California culinary schools, treats cooking as an art by using food as the medium to please the palate as well as to delight the eye. Maldaner's is really two restaurants:

Maldaner's Downstairs, which serves lunch and inexpensive-to-moderate-priced dinners Monday through Friday, and Maldaner's Upstairs, which serves moderate to expensive cuisine Tuesday through Saturday. Although Higgins is the chef upstairs, he helps develop the menu downstairs, and from time to time, some of his upstairs creations can be found on the menu downstairs.

Maldaner's Downstairs
Open: Monday through Friday (during summer Tuesday through Saturday)
11:00 a.m.-9:00 p.m.
Price range: Inexpensive to moderate

Springfield's claim to culinary fame is the "horseshoe," an open-faced sandwich made with toast, a choice of meat, and topped with fries smothered in cheese sauce. Maldaner's version of the horseshoe is better than most because of its crispy homemade fries and its delicious sauce, which is made with sharp cheese mellowed by a touch of beer. Maldaner's serves a number of nicely prepared standard sandwiches such as hamburger, club, BLT, chicken salad, and grilled cheese, but here you can also try something different. The turkey curry sandwich is an excellent example: turkey, Swiss cheese, sweet red onion, and apple slices are bound up in a creamy curry sauce and are grilled between two slices of pumpernickel bread until the bread is crisp and the cheese is melted. Another interesting sandwich is slices of roasted leg of lamb flavored with cilantro, pepper, and garlic served on whole wheat bread. Maldaner's makes wonderful homemade potato chips, so before you order the equally good fries, find out if your sandwich is served with chips. Some of the sandwiches are offered in half portions when you pair them with soup or salad.

Maldaner's makes good salads. The spinach salad is created with very fresh spinach, fresh orange slices, bacon strips, hard-boiled egg wedges, sweet red onions slices, and a nice poppy seed dressing. Other salads offered include a chef, Caesar, and, for the more adventurous, a sesame noodle salad made with noodles and assorted vegetables in a sesame oil and black vinegar dressing.

Dinner at Maldaner's Downstairs can be a little out of the ordinary if you choose. Although you can have a horseshoe, hamburger, or salad for dinner, the menu also features a beef rib eye sandwich with fried onion rings, and an assortment of entrees. Thai chicken cakes with brown rice and peanut sauce is a good entree for those wanting to try a dish influenced by Thai cooking but without the fiery peppers typically used in that cuisine. Two thick patties of shredded chicken, green onion, bread crumbs, and lemony Thai spices are grilled and served with brown rice, a dish of thick peanut sauce with chopped peanuts, and a cucumber salad made with seedless cucumbers, carrots, and a touch of sweet red pepper and cilantro. Another nice entree is the grilled pork chop with Texas-style barbecue sauce and sweet potato pancakes. The thick pork chop is mildly spiced and cooked medium-rare and the accompanying fresh green beans, carrots, and yellow squash make an eye-catching arrangement. The delicious sweet potato pancakes are made with grated sweet potatoes and are fried until golden brown. Other interesting entree possibilities are pan-fried or blackened catfish, grilled yellowfin tuna with garlic mayonnaise and onion rings, pasta carbonara, and roast Cornish game hen with red cabbage and apples.

Each night, diners can expect to find several types of entrees, including a meat-and-vegetable stir-fry, catfish, seafood, at least one type of pasta, and a few other regularly changing entrees. Dinner entrees come with a choice of soup or salad. The dinner salad is basic, and the soups are good; the cream of mushroom is thick with chopped mushrooms.

Dessert at Maldaner's can be a real treat. All are homemade, with some of them making their way downstairs from Maldaner's Upstairs. Desserts change daily, so ask your server about them. The homemade ice cream and sherbert are always good choices.

Maldaner's Upstairs
Open: Tuesday through Saturday
6:00 p.m.-10:00 p.m.
(until 11:00 p.m. Friday and Saturday)
Brunch on Easter Sunday and Mother's Day
Price range: Moderately expensive to expensive
Reservations advised

This simply stated restaurant with its relaxed ambience serves the most creative cuisine in central Illinois. Chef Michael Higgins's style can best be described as "heartland cuisine." He is always challenging himself to develop new recipes that use the season's best local ingredients and stretch the imagination. In his search for balance between the earthy and the ethereal, he is just as at home stuffing quail with lowly cabbage as he is dressing a salad with elegant edible flowers. Although many of his creations are influenced by regional ingredients such as southwestern chiles, Caribbean black beans, or Creole spices, his repertoire has evolved to make use of the best of local ingredients. Higgins grows herbs and edible flowers in his private garden, and hunts for locally grown wild mushrooms, asparagus, and watercress in his creative quest. A meal cooked by Higgins is an adventure worth taking.

Always imaginative, pasta appetizers offer an exciting way to begin a meal. Pasta tossed with smoked duck, pine nuts, green onions, cranberry cream, and melted Asiago cheese successfully combines a number of powerful flavors for a completely unique taste. Another pasta dish redolent with the earthy flavors of fresh chanterelle mushrooms, roasted eggplant, duck, and vegetables in a sauce of chopped fresh tomatoes is excellent. Other wonderful appetizer creations include grilled chicken-jalapeno sausage served with mushroom-stuffed ravioli and a tangy lemon sauce; delicate crab cakes with roasted red pepper sauce, black bean salsa, and jicama salad decorated with the peppery edible leaf of a nasturtium; deep-fried soft-shell crabs in a spicy Creole sauce served with light and creamy garlic mashed potatoes; and warm goat cheese-stuffed phyllo pastry in a roasted red pepper sauce.

Black bean and lamb chili, listed as a soup, is another excellent choice.

The dining adventure continues with inventive and delicious entrees. Perfectly grilled veal tenderloin with chanterelle mushrooms in a sauce of veal stock and cabernet is served with a medallion of cheese-flavored polenta and lightly cooked cubed zucchini, eggplant, and red pepper. Roast chicken--boned and stuffed with a rich mousse of duck and sun-dried tomatoes, then shaped to resemble a huge drumstick-- is glazed with an intensely flavored shitake mushroom sauce and served atop a bed of grilled onions and garnished with crisp, sweet pea pods. Delicate Norwegian salmon is encrusted with the sweet-nutty flavor of pistachios and served with asparagus stir-fried in a rich, soy-based sauce with black mushrooms. Moist quail is paired with the robust flavors of cabbage and pancetta (Italian bacon) and served in a natural sauce. Other possibilities might be rack of lamb grilled over hickory wood with an oriental barbecue sauce and sweet potato fries; roast duck breast stuffed with dates, prunes, and walnuts, and served with wild rice; or grilled grouper with grilled tomatoes, and topped with a green-chile-and-avocado salsa.

Maldaner's ever-changing menu retains certain favorites, such as beef Wellington, the house specialty of prime beef baked with mushroom duxelles in pastry and served with Madeira wine sauce, and aged prime steaks served with sauces such as tomato bearnaise or herb butter. The menu always has at least one veal, chicken, game, fish, and lamb entree, but the way in which they are prepared is constantly changing.

Desserts at Maldaner's are homemade. Always on the menu is the deservedly popular Queen of Sheba, a smooth and rich flourless chocolate cake flavored with brandy and glazed with chocolate ganache. The creme brulee and bread pudding are uninspired, but an apricot-raspberry cobbler, with its rich and crumbly crust and natural fresh-fruit tartness, is an excellent choice. Another wonderful selection is the semisweet chocolate paté, which yields a delicate hint of orange. It is served with vanilla creme Anglaise and sprinkled with toasted hazelnuts. Not to be ignored in the choice of desserts, some of which are presented on a rolling cart, is the homemade ice cream. Ask what flavors are available, and don't assume that you will be depriving yourself of the complex flavors of some of the other desserts. Maldaner's ice cream can be amazing.

Two times a year, on Easter and on Mother's Day, Maldaner's serves Sunday brunch. This is a spectacular meal, with three buffet tables from which you can choose, and choose, and choose! Five or six hot items of chicken, beef, and fish; cold table dishes such as tuna tartar, salmon mousse, and smoked trout; as well as homemade rolls, muffins, and breads; and a fantastic selection of desserts make these occasions a perfect time to sample the diversity of Chef Michael Higgins's talents.

Maldaner's has some very good wines, but you might not know it from looking at the list since vintages are not listed and some wines are not on the list. Ask the hostess for more information if you like.

Monty's Submarine Sandwiches
3124 Montvale Dr.
(217) 546-3020
Open: Daily
11:00 a.m.-10:00 p.m. (noon-8:00 p.m. Sunday)
Price range: Inexpensive

Tucked away in a strip mall is Monty's, a sub-shop with a difference. Monty's huge sandwiches are built on whole wheat rolls (or white rolls if you prefer) and are warmed in an oven-- not a microwave. Especially good are the El Italiano sub with ham, spicy Genoa salami, provolone cheese, lettuce, tomato, mild onion slices, and creamy Italian dressing, and the meatball sub, which is stuffed with spicy meatballs and a tangy tomato sauce. Other subs have turkey, ham, beef, tuna, cheese, or a combination of ingredients. Monty's also has salads and specialty party subs that should be ordered in advance.

New Leaf Deli and Espresso
501 W. Washington
(217) 523-4300
Open: Tuesday through Saturday
11:00 a.m.-3:00 p.m.
5:00 p.m.-8:00 p.m. (Friday and Saturday only)
Price range: Inexpensive to moderate
Reservations required for dinner

Vegetables, beans, and grains take center stage in this '90s version of a healthfood restaurant and coffee house. The New Leaf is not a vegetarian restaurant--there are chicken and tuna items on the menu--but you might well feel that you've done something good for yourself after eating here, and you won't feel the least bit deprived. The restaurant is in a nice old house and features the artwork of local artists such as George Colin and Charles Houska.

The lunch menu consists of soups, unusual salads, sandwiches, and homemade desserts. Regular salads on the menu are brie and fruit salad; tabbullah salad made with bulgar wheat, chopped tomatoes, and parsley and served with pita bread and fruit; tortellini salad; and New Leaf salad, a vegetable salad with sprouts and seeds. The dressing choices are raspberry vinaigrette, herb yogurt, lemon tahini, and Dijon mustard. Sandwiches are served on your choice of a croissant, or wheat, French, or pita bread. The creamy curried chicken salad made with almonds and grapes is very good.

Dinner at the New Leaf is by candlelight. You must call for dinner reservations. The menu is limited to two or three specials. Some possibilities are spinach pasta with clam sauce; Cuban-style chicken breasts with black beans and fried bananas; or vegetable lasagna. The New Leaf features homebaked pies, and a variety of teas and interesting beverages.

Popeye's Bar-B-Q
1100 Martin Luther King Dr.
(217) 522-0386
Open: Daily
10:30 a.m.-9:30 p.m. (until 10:30 p.m. Saturday)
Sunday 1:00 p.m.-7:00 p.m. for take-out only
Price range: Inexpensive

Benson "Popeye" Jones is the third in four generations in the Bar-B-Q business. The business' odyssey began in 1873 in Marion, Louisiana, and moved on to Little Rock, Arkansas, then to Chicago and St. Louis and ended up in Springfield in 1969. Bar-B-Q ribs, rib-tips, pork, beef, chicken, and hot links are on the menu. Delicious original Louisiana inspired Bar-B-Q sauce smothers the meat, which is served on sliced white bread for mopping up the sauce. You have a choice of mild, medium, or hot sauce. Dinners include a good side order of creamy coleslaw and sweet baked beans, which can be ordered separately as well. Popeye's has a drive-up window for take-out orders.

Tokyo of Japan
517 S. 4th St.
(217) 789-7744
Open: Daily
Monday through Friday 11:30 a.m.-2:00 p.m. and 5:00 p.m.-
10:00 p.m. (until 11:00 p.m. Friday and Saturday) and Sunday
4:30 p.m.-9:30 p.m.
Price Range: Moderate
Reservations: Advisable

Tokyo of Japan is one of the most overlooked restaurants in Springfield--and it is open for dinner on Sunday--a time when many restaurants close. At Tokyo of Japan, fresh food is prepared at your table in the centuries-old Teppan-style, and if your chef is in the mood, you will be treated to a spectacle of your chef's skill with a knife. Complete dinners include soup, salad, a shrimp appetizer, an entree, vegetables, rice, and hot tea. The food is very fresh: it has to be--you'd see if it wasn't! Soup and salad are brought to your table from the kitchen. The onion soup is a mild broth with sliced onions and "french fried" onions. The salad is pretty basic, but it has a good and unusual ginger dressing.

The special part of the dinner begins when the chef comes to your table with his cart laden with fresh food that he will stir-fry before your eyes. Each person receives a bowl of rice and two sauces served in individual shallow bowls. The sweet and sour sauce is for seafood, and the hot mustard sauce is for beef and chicken. The meal begins with tasty morsels of shrimp. The sea scallops are an excellent choice: golden brown and crisp on the outside, tender and succulent on the inside. The chicken, prepared in bite-sized pieces, is tender and flavorful. The steak, also cut into bite-sized pieces, is cooked to your order and served with fresh mushrooms. A mound of fresh seasonal vegetables is grilled at the table. The combination of zucchini and cabbage cooked until just crisp is very good. The chef serves each dish as it is done, finishing his service with vegetables. Then he departs leaving you to eat your meal with wooden chop sticks or a fork. Hot tea is also served with the meal.

Tokyo of Japan has children's dinners (available on weekdays) for about half the price of a regular dinner, and they include ice cream. Alcohol is served as are strangely named liquor and fruit-juice concoctions. Ice cream or fruit is available for dessert.

Asian Food Market
947 S. Spring
(217) 523-9005
Open: Daily
10:00 a.m.-7:00 p.m. (Sunday noon-6:00 p.m.)

The Asian Food Market has a huge selection of imported foods items from more than a dozen countries, among them Japan, India, Pakistan, Taiwan, China, Thailand, Vietnam, Korea, Hong Kong, Singapore, the Philippines, Portugal, Costa Rica, and England. It also has a small selection of unusual produce most often used in Asian cooking, and refrigerator and freezer cases of meats, fish, prepared appetizers, egg rolls, vegetables, and other items. Some of the items you can find on the shelves are spices, nuts, beans, noodles, rice, dried mushrooms, dried fish, tea, canned fruits, canned vegetables, candies, cookies, and every kind of Asian food sauce imaginable. A few cooking utensils are also available.

Food Fantasies
1512 W.Wabash
(217) 793-8009
Open: Daily
9:00 a.m.-8:00 p.m. (until 6:00 p.m. Saturday and from
1:00 p.m.-5:00 p.m. Sunday)

Food Fantasies is not the decadent food shop that its name implies; rather, it is a natural and gourmet specialty foods market with a bakery. It is here that people with special dietary concerns can find the food they need. But Food Fantasies has grown into much more than that. Hard-to-find ethnic spices and food items, frozen meals, gourmet foods, body-care products, nutritional supplements, honey-sweetened ice cream, dairy products and dairy substitutes, as well as books, magazines, natural pet food and environmentally sound cleaning products are available. It has a bulk section that includes grains, nuts, herbs and spices, pastas, dried fruits, and coffees.

The bakery produces some "healthy" items such as fruit pies made with canola oil crust and sweetened with fruit juice, whole wheat bread, and corn-based pioneer bread. It also bakes muffins, scones, cookies, and cakes, some of which use sugar. On Friday, you can buy very good challah, the traditional Jewish braided egg bread. Not all items are baked every day, but the bakery will take special orders.

Mel-O-Cream Donuts
217 E. Laurel (217)544-4644
1814 Adlai Stevenson Dr. (217) 529-0046
1953 W. Monroe (217) 546-4651
525 N. Grand Ave. E.(217) 528-2303
Open: Daily
Each shop has different hours. All are open by 6:30 a.m. every
day. Call for specifics.

It's no wonder that Mel-O-Cream Donuts has been in business in Springfield since 1932--the donuts are top notch.

Made fresh daily, the 50 varieties of donuts have a fresh, never oily taste. Mel-O-Cream makes the three basic styles of do- nuts--yeast, cake, and egg--and then tops them or stuffs them with various coatings and fillings. Tropical oils and animal fat are not used in frying these donuts. The most popular donut is the glazed bread donut, but the glazed old-fashioned is also really good.

The Panhandler Shop
1650 Wabash (in the Yard Shopping Center)
(217) 546-6202
Open: Monday through Saturday
10:00 a.m.-6:00 p.m. (until 8:00 p.m. on Friday and 5:00 p.m. on Saturday)

The Panhandler is primarily a gourmet cookware shop. It is the place to look for hard-to-find bakeware, such as imported tart pans. It also has a small selection of specialty food items, chocolates, teas, and coffees.

Pease's Candy Shops
State and Laurel (217) 523-3721
1828 Stevenson Dr. (217) 529-3331
Sangamon Center North Shopping Mall (217) 528-2810
Open: Daily (closed Sunday at Stevenson Dr. location)
All are open daily by 10:00 a.m. Call for specifics

Pease's candy makes a great authentic Springfield gift. The candy company has been in Springfield since 1930 and is still making quality fresh chocolates and coated nuts. Pease's caramels are made with butter and cream and come wrapped in paper, chocolate covered, or in Raggedy Anns. Pease's makes a full line of light, dark, and white chocolate candies. You can buy assorted creams, cherry cordials with and without liqueur, nut clusters, bonbons, chocolate mints, lentils, white chocolate bark, chocolate macadamia nuts, as well as novelty molded chocolates such as golf balls, cars, tennis rackets, and animal lollipops. The coated nuts have a salty yet sweet coating. The caramel apples, available in September and October, are good, and the chocolate-covered strawberries are a real treat.

Springfield Special Events

The Gourmand Experience
Presented by the Central Illinois Culinary Art Association

Each year Springfield is host to an extraordinary culinary event. The Central Illinois Culinary Art Association presents its annual fundraiser called Gourmand Experience. Various member chefs from around Central Illinois prepare something for a five-course dinner. This is an event where chefs who cook plain meals most of the time get to show off their culinary skills and really shine, and chefs who work for private clubs get to dazzle the general public. Some of the chefs who participate in the event are Leland Ball, William Ballard, Robert Snow, and Barb Wall of the Country Club of Decatur; Udo Drier of Willow Knolls Country Club of Peoria; Rick Voudrie of First of America Bank; Mike Higgins and Nancy Howard Higgins of Maldaner's; David Radwine and Earl Uber of the Sangamo Club; Darren Best and Raven Pulliam of Sangamon State University; Maureen Egizii of the Springfield Hilton; and Matt Feges and Timothy Young from a private catering service in Champaign. The event is held in a large dining room at a hotel or university, and the seating is casual, giving participants a chance to meet other food lovers. Some of the food at the dinner is really outstanding, and there is so much of it and the tickets are so reasonably priced that this is an event worth watching for. For the past several years, there has been an hors d'oeurve buffet followed by soup, salad, appetizer, main course, and, finally, a dessert buffet. The hors d'oeuvre buffet is magnificent. Among the selections at previous dinners were Brie en croute, poached whole salmon, marinated mussels with baby shrimp, puff pastry filled with chicken or seafood salad, marinated cheese, cold asparagus, vegetables in aspic, sweet and sour meatballs, a variety of patés, quiche, cheese spinach pies, phyllo-dough meat pies with peanut sauce, seafood salad, and fresh fruits and vegetables. A butter peacock with an asparagus tail graced the buffet table as did beautifully carved ice sculptures.

However tempting the soup and salad might be, if past dinners are any indication, there is so much food still to come that they might be worth just tasting. The appetizer is usually a seafood-based dish such as one year's selection of shrimp lasagna with two sauces, bechamel and tomato. The tender lasagna was sprinkled with crunchy hazelnuts and sliced asparagus. A refreshing sorbet is served between courses to clean the palate and is a nice touch. Each table has a basket of fresh assorted rolls, which might include croissants, pecan rolls, and orange rolls. The dessert buffet offers more than a dozen selections, some of which are excellent. This event is usually held in April. Watch for news of it in the newspaper, or drop a note to the ACF Central Illinois Culinary Art Association, P.O. Box 4385, Springfield, 62709. By all means, don't miss it.

The Joy of Not Cooking
Planned Parenthood Springfield Area

Planned Parenthood's annual fundraiser is a silent auction of food items, including everything from restaurant gift certificates to homemade specialties donated by of some of Springfield's best cooks. This is your chance to buy a Cajun feast, a Lithuanian dinner, an Ethiopian dinner, a West African dinner, Hawaiian barbecued ribs, a New-York-style brunch, a macrobiotic meal, a blue-ribbon fruit pie, a hummingbird cake, or one of a dozen different cheesecakes from the two hundred or so donations to this auction. The highest bidder makes arrangements to pick-up, receive, or in some cases have dinner with the donor. To receive a copy of the catalog, which is available in March, call 544-2744.

Sangamon State University theme dinners

Throughout the year, in conjunction with auditorium shows and World Affairs Council programs, the Sangamon State University kitchen will prepare theme buffet dinners. Some of the international dinners can be quite good. The Irish buffet before the performance of the Irish Rovers had a variety of typical Irish food: two types of salads, including an unusual sausage and tomato salad; two main courses, including Hiberian Hodge-Podge Stew with beef and crisp chunks of carrots, onions, and celery, and--you guessed it--corned beef and cabbage; three vegetables, including brussels sprouts with chestnuts, and peas with mushrooms, cream and nutmeg; delicious Irish soda bread; and an assortment of desserts. Other dinners might include Mexican, Cuban, Cajun, German, Russian, or African. For information see *On Stage*, Sangamon State University's preview of events publication, or call 786-6160 for more information.

Sullivan

Jibby's
119 N. Main
(217) 728-9031 or 728-7112
Open: Monday through Saturday
11:00 a.m.-9:00 p.m. (until 10:00 p.m. Friday and Saturday)
Price range: Inexpensive to moderate

Jibby's is an institution in Sullivan, and its history is linked with the wonderful Little Theatre on the Square, a live theater that graces this small town. Although a tavern, it is quite well suited for taking children for lunch after a matinee performance of the summer children's theater. Ceiling fans keep the smoke under control. Jibby's is known for its steaks, but its menu is a large one that includes pizza, sandwiches, Italian entrees, fish and seafood, chicken, and ribs.

The hamburgers are very good. The "little Jibby" is a one-quarter pound grilled patty and the "big Jibby" is a one-half pound patty served on an onion roll. If you want your burger cooked a certain way, be specific or it will be cooked medium-well. The deluxe beef is a tasty sandwich on a garlic bun filled with beef slices, grilled sweet peppers and onions, and covered with melted mozzarella cheese. All sandwiches are served with chips, pepperoncini, a pickle, and lettuce and onions.

Another good and filling menu item is the crispito: two deep-fried beef-filled burritos, that are topped with chili, tomatoes, onions, and cheddar cheese. Although deep-fried, the flour tortillas used in the burritos were not greasy, and the chili was a good thin-type with beans that did not smother or overpower the burritos.

Sullivan Bakery
9 S. Main
(217) 728-4721
Open: Tuesday through Saturday
5:30 a.m.-4:00 p.m. (until 8:00 p.m. Friday and Saturday during theater season)

What a pleasant surprise this bakery is! Instead of the usual dull bread and dry cookies found at so many small-town bakeries, the bakery was recently purchased by Barb Woolsey who trained at culinary school in South Carolina and then came home to Sullivan. So, along with the usual assortment of cookies, rolls, breads, and cakes, Barb is baking scones, croissants, tarts, eclairs, and challah (braided egg bread), sourdough white and rye breads, dill rolls, and other delectables.

The croissants are buttery and flaky. The raisin and blueberry scones have bits of orange peel, giving them a tangy flavor. Raspberry scones, made with whole wheat flour and fresh raspberries, are delicate and surprisingly light. Delicious pecan tarts have a sweet buttery flavor and lots of fresh pecans in a good pastry. The eclairs are outstanding--filled with a mixture of custard and chantilly (vanilla-flavored whipped cream), the moist, but not soggy, shells are glazed in bittersweet chocolate. The challah is good and very pretty with a sprinkling of poppy seeds over a shiny egg glaze. The dill rolls are a very good light dinner roll with lots of dill and red onion bits.

The bakery is small, so certain items are available only on certain days, but if you call in advance, you can special order what you want or find out what seasonal specialties are available for special order.

Taylorville

Aunt Sophie's
207 W. Main Cross
(217) 824-6711
Open: Monday through Saturday
7:00 a.m.-6:00 p.m. (Saturday until 4:00 p.m.)
Price range: Inexpensive

Aunt Sophie's is a cute deli with a green awning just off the main square in downtown Taylorville. It offer's the usual assortment of cold cuts, meat salads, and cheeses to make fresh sandwiches. It also offers nice homemade soups, such as chicken noodle soup featuring homemade noodles and bits of chicken, celery, and carrots. The service is simple--plastic dishware, not china--but the food is fresh and the atmosphere pleasant.

A homemade dessert special is featured each week, in addition to regular commercially prepared desserts. The German chocolate upside-down cake is really good with a moist chocolate bottom, creamy caramel middle, and crispy toasted coconut and nut topping.

Aunt Sophie's has a take-out deli counter and an old-fashioned glass case with glass jars of candy sold in bulk. It also has flavored popcorn in almost a dozen flavors.

Mi Casa Mexican Restaurant and Cantina
301 N. Main
(217) 287-2303
Open: Daily
11:00 a.m.-9:00 p.m (until 10:00 p.m. Friday and Saturday)
Price range: Inexpensive

Since September of 1991, those of us who love Mexican food have had something to celebrate: Mi Casa Mexican Restaurant and Cantina opened in Taylorville. This unpretentious and friendly restaurant serves authentic homemade Mexican food. The menu is large, offering a choice of ten appetizers and an assortment of entrees, including familiar dishes such as tacos, enchiladas, and burritos, as well as more unusual items such as *chili rellenos*, chicken in *mole* (chocolate) sauce, and pork in *verde* (green) sauce. The guacamole gave us the first hint that we were on to something special. Although a simple salad, guacamole can be tricky to make because its main ingredient, avocados, must be ripe but not bruised or stringy. Mi Casa's wonderful guacamole is made with perfectly ripe avocado chunks, tomatoes, onions, and a touch of fresh cilantro; it is creamy and delicate. You won't find it listed under appetizers; instead look on the list of side dishes. Don't miss Mexican *chorizo con queso fundido*. Made with the restaurant's homemade spicy chorizo sausage, melted Monterey Jack and chopped jalapeno peppers and served with freshly fried corn tortilla chips, this appetizer is spicy, gooey, and delicious.

Mi Casa's list of entrees is extensive with combination plates that allow you to sample a variety of dishes. The chili rellenos is a great choice--tasty fresh poblano peppers filled with Monterey Jack cheese are dipped in batter, deep-fried, and covered with a spicy tomato sauce that has chunks of onions, green peppers, and green olives. The enchiladas in mole sauce are not ordinary enchiladas. These have large chunks of fresh chicken (or beef) in a very special sauce made with chocolate, chilies, and spices. Entrees are served with delicious refried beans, made fresh with chorizo sausage and topped with melted cheese, and Mexican rice that is cooked in a tomato-based sauce with fresh vegetable pieces; shredded lettuce, chopped tomatoes, and fresh flour or corn tortillas also comes with the meal. Other entrees include seven variations of steak, homemade pork tamales, spicy hot chili, taco or seafood salads, Mexican-style catfish, and, for the timid, a few American-style entrees.

Mi Casa has some nice desserts. The Mexican fried ice cream is a special treat for children. Served in a fried taco shell, this cube of vanilla ice cream has a deep-fried, crunchy, Rice-Crispy-like coating and is served with chocolate or strawberry sauce. Cream cheese adds an unusual flavor to Mi Casa's version of traditional Mexican flan (molded custard in caramel sauce). Bunuelos (deep-fried pastries sprinkled with cinnamon and sugar) are traditional New Year's treats that you can try here anytime. Mi Casa has Mexican beer and a selection of other imported beers, and offers tequila margaritas by the glass or pitcher. Despite the availability of liquor, Mi Casa is a family restaurant that welcomes children.

Tuscola

Spicery Tea Room
101 E. Scott
(217) 253-5091
Open: Monday through Saturday
10:00 a.m.-2:00 p.m.
Price range: Inexpensive

Shop 'til you drop at the gigantic Four Seasons clothing store and then relax over lunch at the cozy Spicery Tea Room. Decorated in lace and flowered wallpaper, the tea room serves homemade food that is both tasty and comforting. The Spicery is located in a rare prefabricated Sears and Roebuck house that in 1909 was shipped to Tuscola by railroad and then assembled by local contractors.

The menu features items that are low in calories and fat and still taste good. Typical tea room offerings--nice salads, soups, and casserole meals--come with homebaked breads or muffins and a salad with a homemade dressing. Also typical of tea room fare is the good selection of fresh teas (hot or iced), and decadent desserts. The house salad is pretty standard, but it has a tangy poppy seed dressing. The turkey-bake casserole is served with moist, sweet poppy seed bread and garnished with fresh fruit. A good choice, it is light and tasty, with lots of turkey and asparagus, and topped with Swiss cheese.

The house pie, chocolate pecan pie, is served warm with a Hershey-type chocolate sauce. The filling is low on pecan flavor and couldn't stand on its own as a pecan pie, but if chocolate is your passion, this pie will do. Also available are chocolate cheesecake, fudge cake, lemon dream pie, and French silk pie. The iced tea is good and plentiful.

Williamsville

Brennan's Cafe
100 W. Main St.
(217) 566-2035
Open: Daily
6:00 a.m.-7:00 p.m. (9:00 a.m.-1:00 p.m. weekends)
Price range: Inexpensive

Weary travelers can stop at Brennan's Cafe for a hot, inexpensive meal and, if they're in the mood, for a little conversation. A communal table in the back of the restaurant where local farmers eat welcomes strangers. The lunch and dinner menu includes full meals of catfish, carp, steaks, chicken, and more, and there are sandwiches and daily specials. The ponyshoe, a smaller version of the horseshoe, is really large enough for all but the biggest appetite. It has a creamy, mild cheese sauce. A decent piece of fruit pie rounds out a meal in this cute, local restaurant.

Farm-Fresh Products

Fruits
Vegetables
Turkeys
Chickens
Beef
Maple Syrup
Honey
Nuts
and more

Arenzville

Vanderpool Orchard
R.R. 1, Box 148
(217) 997-5851
Open: May through November
Monday, Wednesday, Friday, Saturday
8:00 a.m.-5:00 p.m. (call for Sunday U-pick hours)

Vanderpool Orchard has U-Pick and some ready-picked strawberries, cherries, plums, peaches, and apples. The strawberries begin in mid-May, the cherries in early June, the peaches in late June, the plums in mid-July, and the apples in late summer and fall. Vanderpool has black raspberries and blackberries already-picked available in late June and July. This orchard has the following varieties of apples: Lodi, Earliblaze, Gala, Ozark Gold, Jonalicious, Jonathan, Golden Delicious, Red Delicious, Blushing Golden, and Winesap. Call ahead for ready-picked fruit. Vanderpool makes its own non-preservative apple cider and raw honey sold either strained or in the honeycomb.

Athens

Frank Farms, Inc. (asparagus, sweet corn)
R.R. 2-Box 41
(217) 636-8590
Open: Call for times and availability

At the Frank Farms, you can pick your own or buy ready-picked asparagus beginning in late April or early May. The Franks also sell sweet corn in July and evergreen wreaths, roping, and trees before Christmas. Call to be sure someone will be home and for directions to the farm.

Bloomington and Normal

The Apple Barn
R.R. 4, Box 94
Bloomington
(309) 963-5557
July through November or December
Open: Monday through Saturday
8:00 a.m.-5:00 p.m. (Sunday from 9:00 a.m. in peak season)

With 6,000 apple trees, the Apple Barn is the largest apple orchard in central Illinois. Not only does it have a large variety of apples, this orchard also has a shop in which fresh baked goods such as muffins, cookies, donuts, apple cakes, and pies, and cheese, sausages, and wicker baskets are sold along with apples, cider, and apple butter. Some of the apple varieties available at the Apple Barn are Lodi, Gala, Earliblaze, Empire, Grimes Golden, Jonamac, Paula Red, Prima, Ozark Gold, Cortland, Jonathan, Golden Delicious, Red Delicious, Stamen, Firmgold, Rome, and Granny Smith.

The Apple Barn is host to two festivals. A crafts show is held the weekend before Labor Day and a huge Harvest Day Celebration occurs in October, at which there are craft demonstrations, musicians, food, and apples galore. Visitors to the fairs can park in the 10-acre parking lot and await the wagon shuttle to take them to the fair. The Apple Barn is five miles west of Bloomington.

Brighton

McAdams Orchard
R.R. 2, Box 62012
(618) 372-8968
Open: Mid-May through October
Daily
9:00 a.m.-5:00 p.m.
(from 1:00 p.m. Sunday)
Dawn until dusk
for berry picking

The McAdams Orchard has a spectacular variety of fruit, including red, yellow, purple, and black raspberries; gooseberries; elderberries; blackberries; 15 varieties of peaches; nectarines; apricots; plums; red and yellow sweet cherries; sour cherries; and more than 30 varieties of apples. In addition, there is asparagus, sweet corn, tomatoes, peppers, squash, and pumpkins. The season begins around mid-May, when asparagus is for sale ready-picked. The berries begin around mid-June and are everbearing, so they are available into September. Berries are sold U-pick, but some can be special ordered. The apples are U-pick and include some of the following varieties: Paula Red, Gala, Mollie's Delicious, Red Delicious, Yellow Delicious, Empire, Blushing Golden, Jonagold, Firmgold, Jonalicious, Ozark Gold, Grimes Golden, Newtown Pippin, Mutsu, Spigold, Northern Spy, Fuji, York Imperial, Granny Smith, and Arkansas Black.

The McAdamses have a barn store from which they sell fresh produce and their own apple cider, which has no preservatives. Call for the availability of berries. To get there go one mile east of Brighton on Brown Road and then south one mile on Seminary Road to Orchard and Market.

Buffalo Hart

Jeff Nelson (asparagus)
R.R. 1, Box 172A
(217) 364-4899
Open: Mid-April for eight weeks
Evenings and week-ends

Beginning around mid-April and for the next eight weeks, you can pick your own asparagus or buy it already-picked from this four-acre plot. In addition to green asparagus, Jeff Nelson is growing a small amount of white asparagus. The address is Buffalo because there is no post office in Buffalo Hart, but Nelson's place is in Buffalo Hart, which is halfway between Springfield and Lincoln. Call for information on availability.

The Berry Patch (asparagus, berries, and pumpkins)
R.R. 1, Box 173
(217) 364-5606
Open: Late April through October
Daily in strawberry season
6:00 a.m. to dusk in strawberry season, at other times call

Although it is known mainly for berries, the Berry Patch starts the season with asparagus, which is usually available by special order ready-picked at the end of April for four to six weeks. Around Memorial Day strawberries are ripe and ready for U-pick for about two or three weeks. They can be special ordered by calling in advance. Red raspberries and thornless blackberries ripen next, around mid-July, and are available for U-pick or ready-pick. The blackberries last about three weeks; and the red raspberries, which last for two weeks, also have a second crop in August that continues until a killing frost. In late September and October, you can pick your own Jack-O-Lantern and mini-pumpkins. Call ahead for picking days and times.

Carlinville

Broom Orchard
R.R. 4
(217) 854-3514
Open: Mid-May through Christmas
Daily9:00 a.m.-6:00 p.m.

At Broom Orchard the season starts with strawberries, which are available in May or June. The three-acre strawberry patch is primarily a U-pick operation, but the Brooms will take special orders if called in advance. The 5,000-tree apple orchard also has some peach and nectarine trees, which begin to bear fruit in late July to mid-August if the weather is good.

Broom's is known for its excellent cider, which it makes fresh beginning on Labor Day. Although the orchard grows mostly Jonathan, Red Delicious, and Golden Delicious apples, the Brooms are branching out with some interesting varieties such as Gala, Grimes Golden, Empire, Mutsu, Granny Smith, and Blushing Golden.

The Broom family is host to two annual fall events: an apple festival held the fourth ("or thereabouts") weekend in September and a pumpkin festival held in mid-October. At the apple festival you can pick your own apples, browse at a crafts exhibit, listen to local musicians, and buy lunch provided by the Macoupin County pork or beef producers. Similar activities await visitors to the pumpkin festival, but the main draw is the eight-acre pumpkin patch, from which children get to choose their own pumpkins.

The retail store on the premises is open every day from strawberry season until Christmas. Here you can buy cider, apple butter, B-B-Q sauce, honey, jams and jellies, mulling spices, relish, popcorn, holiday fruit baskets, and Christmas trees. Also available are cute, red wooden apple necklaces and earrings that would make great gifts for your favorite teacher. To get there, drive west on Rt. 108 to the Amtrak station, go 2½ miles, and look for the sign on the left.

Malham Orchard
R.R. 4, Box 197
(217) 854-2815
Mid-June through December
Daily
9:00 a.m.-6:00 p.m.

Purple raspberries start the fruit season at Malham Orchard in mid to late-June. The raspberries, which are a cross between red and black raspberries, can be purchased ready-picked or you can pick them yourself.

In early or mid-August, if the weather has been kind, Malham's 400 nectarine and peach trees begin to bear fruit. Picked ripe, the nectarines are golden in color with lots of red blush. Their flesh is bright yellow and wonderfully sweet-tart.

Malham's has Glohaven peaches, a freestone variety with sweet yellow flesh, and Jubilee, a smaller peach--similar to a white peach--with a subtle sweet flavor and a very fuzzy skin. Nectarines and peaches grown elsewhere, picked before they are ripe and sold in grocery stores, simply cannot compare to these. They are almost exotic in their novelty and well worth the effort to get them.

Malham's has 22 varieties of apples. Some are available as early as the peaches in August. Early apples are Prima and Paula Red; Empire, Mollie's Delicious, Ozark Gold, and Gala are usually not far behind. Ripening somewhat later are Jonathan, Red and Yellow Delicious, Blushing Golden, York Imperial, Willow Twig, Newtown Pippin, Granny Smith, Virginia Winesap, among other varieties. Apples are picked through mid-October and sold until they run out, usually in February. Apple cider is made on the premises. Malham's excellent cider won first place in the 1991 Illinois Horticulture Society Competition. The cider is made both with and without preservatives.

The retail store at this 5,000-tree apple orchard also sells honey, sorghum, no-sugar apple butter, and locally grown produce, such as tomatoes and sweet corn, when available. In October, pumpkins and squash grown at Malham's are for sale. To get there, drive west on Rt. 108 to the Amtrak station, go two and a half miles, cross the railroad tracks, and look for the sign.

Champaign and Urbana

Curtis Orchard
R.R. 2, 3902 S. Duncan Rd.
Champaign
(217) 359-5565
Open: August 1 through December 20
Daily
9:00 a.m.-5:30 p.m. (noon to 5:00 p.m. Sunday)

This large, 5,000-tree apple orchard has 30 varieties of apples including Paula Red, Gala, Jonathan, Empire, McIntosh, Red Delicious, Golden Delicious, Jonamac, Ozark Gold, Arkansas Black, Northern Spy, Mutsu, Jonagold, Braeburn, Fuji, Granny Smith, Rome, Winesap, Stamen Winesap, and Criterion. The major varieties are available for U-pick and other varieties are available ready-picked. Ready-picked and U-pick red raspberries are ripe in August. Concord grapes, plums, squash, and gourds can be bought U-pick or ready-picked. Cider is made in the fall.

A petting zoo with goats, horses, rabbits, and chickens makes this a great place to take children, and in the fall children can pick out their own pumpkins from the large pumpkin patch, play in the straw maze and straw jump, and enjoy cider donuts and caramel apples as well. Curtis Orchard is located on Duncan Road, 3½ miles south of Rt. 10 (Springfield Avenue).

Chapin

Applesource
R.R. 1, Box 94
(217) 245-7589
Open: Daily
Mid-August through Halloween and mail-order until January
8:00 a.m.-sunset

Tom and Jill Vorbeck's unique apple business is one of our local treasures. It has received recognition in the *New York Times* as one of the nation's outstanding mail-order food businesses. Those of us living in Central Illinois are indebted to the Vorbeck's not only for growing and selling more than 100 varieties of apples but also for inspiring other growers in Illinois to take the risk of offering a larger variety of quality fruit.

Applesource has 1,200 trees, including antique apples, rare apples that have been in this country for some time but have not been available outside of private collections, and apples that were developed for marketing by various agricultural experiment stations around the country. For a description of various apples see the Apple Chart on page 121. Some of the varieties grown at Applesource are: Arkansas Black, Blushing Golden, Calville Blanc, Chieftan, Empire, Fuji, Gala, Golden Delicious, Hudson's Golden Gem, Idared, Jonagold, Jonalicious, Jonamac, Jonathan, Lady, Melrose, Mutsu, Ozark Gold, Newtown Pippin, Spartan, Spigold, Sweet Sixteen, Tydeman's Late Orange, and Winter Banana. The Vorbeck's sell apples at their orchard, at the Jacksonville summer farmer's market, and through their catalog business.

Applesource's mail-order apples make wonderful gifts. There are a number of different boxes containing two trays from which to choose. Perhaps the most interesting are the explorer pack and the sampler pack, which contain up to twelve different varieties of apples. For the more adventurous, there is a pick-your-own (PYO) box that allows you to choose up to six varieties from each of the various orchards. The apples are shipped from orchards in California, Michigan, and Indiana, as well as from Applesource. They come in a heavy, nicely decorated box. Call for a copy of the Applesource catalog.

Chatham

Mau Farms (asparagus, raspberries)
R.R. 1 Box 289
(217) 483-4364
Open: April through August
Daily
7:00 a.m.-5:00 p.m (later during season)

Asparagus starts the season in early April at Dan Mau's Farm. It is available ready-picked until mid-June. Black raspberries are ready in mid-June through mid-July. Raspberries are primarily for U-pick, but some special orders will be taken. You can also buy sweet corn ready-picked in mid-July until the beginning of August.

Morrison Hilltop Orchard
R.R. 1-Box 209
(217) 483-2103
Open: End of April through mid-June and mid-July through Thanksgiving
Daily
8:30 a.m.-6:00 p.m. (Sunday 1:00 p.m.-5:30 p.m.)

Beginning around the end of April through mid-June, bedding plants, of both vegetables and flowers, are sold at the roadside stand. The stand closes down for a month until vegetables are ready. Some of the vegetables grown at Morrison's are okra, green beans, tomatoes, sweet peppers, and summer squash. Around late July look for purple raspberries, and in mid to late August the red raspberries are ready. Morrison's has an excellent variety of apples, including Gala, Empire, Red Delicious, Yellow Delicious, Jonathan, Stamen Winesap, Mutsu, Melrose, Arkansas Black, Jonagold, Jonalicious, Blushing Golden, and Newtown Pippin. Pumpkins, winter squash, gourds, Indian corn, apple cider, and mums are also for sale in the fall.

Peterman Farm (berries)
R.R. 1, Box 418-a
(217) 438-6364
Open: End of May through end of August

The Petermans have red raspberries and blackberries to sell ready-picked. The red raspberries, which are available for two or three weeks, start at the end of May or beginning of June with a second crop in mid-August. The blackberries are usually ready around the first week in July and are available for three or four weeks. Call to place your order and for directions to the farm.

Coffeen

Lawrence Farms (berries)
R.R. 1
(217) 534-6330
Open: Mid to late May for three weeks (strawberries) and mid-July until the end of August (blackberries)
Monday through Saturday
7:00 a.m.-7:00 p.m.

Lawrence Farm has four acres of strawberries and one acre of blackberries. It is primarily a U-pick operation, but some special orders will be taken. Call ahead to make sure that strawberries and blackberries are available when you want to pick, and to get directions to the farm.

Colfax

Petersen produce (stoneground wheat, melons, produce)
R.R. 2
(309) 723-4681
Open: June through September
Call to be sure someone is home

The Petersen's wheat is organically grown and ground in a stone mill. Their other produce, although not organically grown, is grown with a minimum of insecticides and no herbicides. They grow fresh herbs, and a variety of melons such as watermelon, honeydew, muskmelon, and crenshaw. Also available are tomatoes, sweet corn, peppers, sweet onions, and U-pick green beans. The Petersens sell their produce on Saturdays at the farmers markets in Champaign and in Normal.

Cowden

Dunaway Berry Farm
R.R. 1
(217) 783-6367
Open: Memorial Day through end of June (or thereabouts)
Monday through Saturday
7:00 a.m. until dusk

Dunaway's has 16 acres of strawberries. You can pick them yourself or call in your order. An irrigation system makes Dunaway's a reliable source of berries, even in a dry season.

The farm is 14 miles from Shelbyville. Call ahead for directions if necessary.

Decatur

Mari-Mann Herbs
North End of St. Louis Bridge Rd.
R.R. 4, Box 7
(217) 429-5400
Open; Every day
9:00 a.m.-5:00 p.m. (from noon on Sunday)

If you stroll through the garden at Mari-Mann herbs you'll find 75 varieties of herbs, everlastings, and wildflowers that are used in the line of Mari-Mann products sold in the shop. Specialty foods and items include dilly dip mix, spoon herbal sauce, salad herb mix, herb salt, gourmet herbal vinegars, jellies, relishes, herbal teas, and custom-made wreaths and decorations. The herbs and everlastings are also dried and sold for craft making. The shop also stocks potpourri and fragrance oils, herbal cosmetics, candles, stationary, candy-making flavorings, a small selection of cookware, biscuits, mixes, and a nice selection of herb and flower books as well as cookbooks.

Throughout the year, Mari-Mann has a variety of cooking classes and demonstrations. A number of classes are taught by Barb Wall, the 1991 winner of the Chef of the Year Award of the Central Illinois Culinary Art Association. Mari-Mann will arrange special teas or lunches with tours of the gardens for groups of 12 or more. Call for more information about classes and special parties.

Eldred

Emerald Valley Pecans
At the Kampsville Ferry
(217) 983-2831 or 945-6397
Open: End of October until
Thanksgiving
Call for availability

Local residents recall the vision of 350-pound "R. B." (Richard Best) perched on his ladder grafting his beloved pecan trees. In the early 1920s, when R. B. came as a farmhand to this piece of land beside the river, he loved the native pecan trees that he found. Later, after he had become a successful corn hybridizer who had accumulated 3,000 acres of rich farmland, he kept 300 acres of pecan trees. Grafting was his hobby, and his grove eventually contained 36 varieties of pecans. Although his family no longer owns the grove, it is the largest pecan grove this far north in the country. Beginning in October or November, after a hard frost or two, the pecans start falling and are ready for "picking" or buying ready-picked. Local residents prefer *major,* the most prolific variety, but Mary Voiles, R. B.'s daughter, prefers the lighter and meatier *peruque.* Illinois pecans are smaller than their southern counterparts, but in a good season they are tastier because of their higher concentration of oil.

You can buy them ready-picked at the blazing white shed with green trim that is on the north side of Rt. 108 at the Kampsville Ferry, or you can pick them yourself and keep one-third and give back two-thirds. Growing pecans this far north is chancy and sometimes the crop is very small, so be sure to call ahead for both availability and the hours of operation.

Fisher

***Chuck's Flower and Garden Center** (asparagus, berries, produce, flowers)*
R.R. 1, Box 51
(217) 897-1127
Open: Year-round
Monday through Saturday
8:00 a.m.-6:00 p.m. (until 5:00 p.m. in winter)

Chuck's has U-pick produce including asparagus in mid-April, strawberries around Memorial Day, and thornless blackberries in August. In addition, it has an unusual variety of other U-pick produce such as sugar-snap peas, sweet peas, green beans, broccoli, cabbage, cucumbers, beets, okra, eggplant, brussels sprouts, and 20 varieties each of peppers and tomatoes, all available throughout their seasons. Chuck's sells bedding plants of flowers, vegetables, and herbs beginning in April and seasonal potted flowers, such as poinsettias, azaleas, lilies, African violets, gloxinias, and primroses throughout the year.

At their roadside stand you can also buy some of the above vegetables as well as rhubarb, sweet corn, and cauliflower, and fruits including peaches, pears, plums, blueberries, cantaloupes, seedless watermelons, and apples. Chuck's is one mile north of Fisher on 1st St. Call for U-pick information.

Gays

Dewar's Berries
R.R. 2, Box 66
(217) 752-6235
Open: July 1 for five to seven weeks
Monday through Saturday
7:00 a.m.-dusk

Blueberries are available from the first of July to early or mid-August because this farm has early, middle, and late varieties of blueberries. The operation is U-pick only. It is located eight miles southwest of Mattoon. Call ahead for availability and directions.

Greenup

Earthborne Farm (organic berries, melons, vegetables, pumpkins)
R.R. 1, Box 298
(217) 923-3035
Open: Mid-May through Halloween
Daily
9:00 a.m.-5:00 p.m.

Terry Holsapple's 120-acre farm has been certified organic by the Organic Crop Improvement Association. The season starts with U-pick organic strawberries in mid-May or early June. Then look for watermelons and muskmelons from mid-July through September. Green peppers and sweet corn are also grown on the farm. Every October, on Friday, Saturday, and Sunday, the farm becomes host to thousands of people who come to pick their own pumpkins from the organic pumpkin patch, find their way out of the straw maze, and go on nightly haunted hay rides.

Grissom Orchards and Cider Mill
R.R. 1, Box 99
(217) 923-3736
Open: July through December
9:00 a.m.-6:00 p.m. daily

This 70-acre orchard has more than 5,000 apple trees and 1,000 peach and nectarine trees. Most interesting is the large variety of apples grown here and late peaches that are available well into September. Apple varieties available include Paulared, Cortland, Gala, Ozark Gold, Jonathan, Red Delicious, Golden Delicious, Granny Smith, Spigold, Esopus Spitzenberg, and Newtown Pippin. The Fayette peaches, a freestone variety, are a special treat so late in the season.

The roadside shop also sells sweet corn, pears, plums, cider, apple butter, peach butter, honey, nuts, pumpkins, cheeses, meats, and other items. It is located one mile north of Greenup on Rt. 130.

Havana

McClure Brothers (vegetables, melons, gladiolus)
R.R. 1, Box 374
(309) 543-2632
Open: July through Halloween

This roadside stand is especially interesting because in addition to selling sweet corn, squash, tomatoes, peppers, beans, cantaloupe, watermelon, pumpkins, Indian corn and other produce, this third generation of McClures raises more than one million gladiolus on 30 acres of their farm. Motorists driving on Rt. 97 in August will be astonished and delighted by the spectacle of the 40 or so different varieties of these majestic flowers. You can stop and buy a bouquet of fresh cut flowers to take home. The McClures also sell gladioli bulbs (called corms) and perennial flower plants such as peonies, liatris, yarrow, baby's breath, and lavender in April or in the fall. If no one is at the stand just wander back to the house and ring the bell.

Kilbourne

Hodgson's Farmstand and Greenhouses (bedding plants, produce)
Box 108
(309) 538-4296
Open: April through October
Daily 7:00 a.m.-8:00 p.m.

In April you can begin buying bedding plants including flowers and herbs. Sweet corn, cantaloupe, watermelon, zucchini, tomatoes, peppers, eggplant, pumpkins, Indian corn, gourds, and popcorn are among the produce available.

Lincoln

Kasa's Produce
R.R. 4
(217) 735-2001
Open: April through November
Dawn until dusk

This market sells fresh produce from its own and from other farms. Some of the seasonal offerings are: asparagus, strawberries, tomatoes, sweet corn, peppers, cucumbers, and pumpkins. Also available are honey, peanuts, gourds, Indian corn, and more. To get there drive about ½ mile east of Lincoln Christian College on Highway 10.

Ott's Honey
906 Peoria
(217) 732-4633
Open: Call to make arrangements for honey

The Otts sell their honey in a few local shops, at flea markets and craft fairs, and from their home. Although it is difficult to determine the exact source, the Otts believe that most of their honey is collected from soybeans. The honey is amber in color and ready in June, July, and August, leading them to believe that their bees have been busy working the local soybean fields. Call for information on availability.

Three Sisters Orchard and Greenhouse
R.R. 3, Box 46 (eight miles south of Lincoln)
(217) 732-9081
Open: Mid-April through November
Call first for directions and availability

This orchard has an interesting variety of fruit trees--3,300 in all. Among them are white peach, yellow peach, apricot, sour cherry, and sweet cherry, all of which begin bearing fruit in June. In the fall look for a variety of apples: Red Delicious, Yellow Delicious, Jonared, and Mutsu, as well as pears. In mid-April you can buy an assortment of vegetable bedding plants such as tomato, cabbage, pepper, broccoli, and cauliflower. Apple cider and freshly ground horseradish are also made here.

Mahomet

Twin Silos Orchard
R.R. 1, Box 130
Open: Mid-August through November
Daily
9:00 a.m.-5:30 p.m. (noon-5:00 p.m. Sunday)

At Twin Silos, red raspberries are available for U-pick (and some special orders) in August, just about the time the early apples begin. Among the apple varieties available at this young 2,000-tree orchard are Gala, Ozark Gold, Empire, Jonathan, Red Delicious, Golden Delicious, Blushing Golden, Mutsu, and Arkansas Black. U-pick Concord grapes are ready in September or October. Twin Silo also makes its own cider (available around Labor Day) and sells honey produced in its own hives. Locally grown gourmet popcorn and jams and jellies are among the other items you can buy at the orchard.

Melvin

Second Nature Farm (organic chickens)
R.R. 1, Box 68
(217) 388-2888
Open: By appointment

At Second Nature Farm chickens are humanely treated and raised without chemicals or antibiotics. Commonly known as organic or free-range chickens, these are fed a diet mainly of corn and soybeans grown without pesticides--and allowed to roam free, producing a leaner chicken. You can buy the chickens processed and frozen at Strawberry Field's Natural Food Market in Champaign, Jerry's IGA on Philo Road in Urbana, or you can have them shipped to you. Call the farm for details about shipping.

Moweaqua

Bohlen's Orchard
(217) 768-4620
Open: Mid-July through October
Call for availability and directions

It is worth the short drive south on Rt. 51 from Decatur to buy apples from Bohlen's Orchard. The Bohlens grow more than 60 varieties of apples. Some are sold from the orchard in Moweaqua and some are sold in Springfield. For a listing of many of the varieties of apples grown here, see the Springfield section.

New Berlin

Buckman's Orchard
R.R. 1, Box 36A
(217) 626-1369
Open: Mid-August
through October
Daily
9:00 a.m.-5:30 p.m.

This 200-tree orchard sells apples and a few pears. The apple varieties are McIntosh; Prima, a large Jonathan cross; Red Delicious; Yellow Delicious; and Arkansas Black. In addition to the apples, Buckman's has three varieties of pears including Magness, a greenish-yellow, slightly russeted pear with a sweet, juicy flesh, and Moonglow, a dull yellow, juicy and fine-textured pear. They make their own apple cider. Call ahead for harvest information and for directions.

Spring Creek Farm (organic eggs and poultry)
R.R. 2
(217) 488-6446
Open: By arrangement

Kathleen Vinehout is an "on-farm egg producer" of chicken, goose, and duck eggs. She also sells live turkeys, chickens, ducks, and geese. Her poultry is raised without antibiotics and is fed locally grown feed. Her chicken eggs come from free-ranging chickens raised on her chemical-free farm. Call her to arrange to purchase eggs or live poultry.

Pana

White Oak Farm (organic beef and produce)
Bear Creek Road, R. R.4
(217) 562-2573
By arrangement for pick-up or delivery

Deonne Orvis raises organic beef for sale locally in small or large quantities and is a farmer in a community-supported agricultural venture. First, the beef. The cattle on the farm are raised on ground that does not have herbicides, pesticides, or synthetic fertilizers. The animals do not receive hormones or preventative antibiotics. Orvis's commitment to the environment is evident in her description of her beef. She says that her cattle are raised with TLC in a small individually named herd; are free within a shaded pasture, creek, and loafing shed with plenty of room for normal social interaction and play; are fed mother's milk, pasture grass, and on-farm grown hay; are lean because they are fed grain only in the coldest months; are grazed on local privately owned land managed for sustainable use; and ride in a private trailer to be butchered three miles from the farm. Surprisingly, many of the beef cuts are comparable in price to store-bought beef. The animals are butchered between November and January and meat is meat is available until it runs out. Phone orders are taken on Thursday and Friday mornings, and you can pick up your order or make arrangements to have it delivered to Springfield or Decatur.

In 1992, Orvis began selling in shares in Community Supported Agriculture (CSA). For approximately $370 each shareholder receives a portion of freshly picked produce from the 70 or so varieties of organically grown vegetables, herbs, fruits, and nuts harvested from mid-May through November. Produce can be picked up at drop-off points in Springfield and Decatur. Call for more information on this exciting venture.

Petersburg

The Shirding Farm (asparagus)
R.R. 2, Box 129
(217) 632-7340
Open: By appointment

In late April or early May, the Shirdings have fresh asparagus to sell. Call ahead to place orders and for directions to the farm.

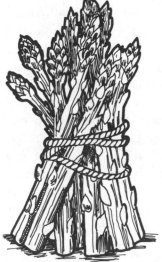

Pleasant Plains

Fromm-Huff Farm (blueberries)
R.R. 2
(217) 626-1583
Open: End of June through July
Tuesday, Wednesday, Thursday, and Saturday
7:00 a.m.-noon (call for availability)

This ten-acre farm has blueberries for U-pick only. Although the farm is open four days a week, it is sometimes closed for a few days to wait for more berries to ripen. Call to hear a recording of the availability of berries before you go picking. To get there from Springfield, take Rt. 97, turn left at the green sign to Pleasant Plains, and watch for Fromm-Huff signs.

Pontiac

Jones Strawberry Woods (berries and pumpkins)
R.R. 3
(815) 998-2585
Open: Mid-April through October 31 (closed in August)
9:00 a.m.-6:00 p.m.
(7:30 a.m.-7:30 p.m. during strawberry season)

Jones Strawberry Woods has much more than ten acres of strawberries: The season starts in mid-April with ready-picked asparagus and bedding plants. Strawberries are available for U-pick and special order beginning the last week in May and lasting for about three weeks. Then come the black raspberries in mid-June, followed by purple raspberries and blueberries around July 1. Blueberries are available for about four weeks. At the beginning of September red raspberries are in full swing and last through September. The 15-acre pumpkin patch at this farm provides for some fun fall festivities. Children can pick their own pumpkin from the pumpkin patch, to which they are delivered on a hayrack, and walk through "Pumpkinland," a wooded area, to see the 100 straw-stuffed painted pumpkin-head characters. Some of the characters children might come upon during this nature walk are Snow White and the seven dwarfs, and other children's story and nursery rhyme characters. The pumpkin festivities begin the third week in September and go through October 31. Hayrack rides are only available on weekends. The farm is located eight miles west of Pontiac on Rt. 116 and five miles north of Graymont.

Rochester

Carol Harp (herbs, produce)
R.R. 1, Box 107
(217) 498-7201
Open: By arrangement

Carol Harp is an organic gardener who sells herbs, sprouts, and fresh vegetables--some even in the dead of winter. Her fresh herbs include chives, Italian parsley, basil, bay laurel, rosemary, sage, thyme, oregano, hyssop, and others. She grows cherry tomatoes, green beans, lettuce, cantaloupe, spinach, cucumbers, and alfalfa sprouts, and is adding a greenhouse that will enable her have a selection of vegetables in the winter. She delivers, so call her for information on availability and to arrange delivery.

Cascade Sheep and Wool Company
R.R. 1, Box 60
(217) 498-7522
Open: By appointment

The Behls sell drug and hormone-free lambs when the lambs are five months old. They will take the lamb to YT packing, where you can arrange to have some of the meat fresh or all of it frozen The smallest quantity you can buy is one-half of a lamb. Call for information about availability.

Sadorus

Herbs of Grace
150 N. County Road 400 E.
(217) 598-2542
Open: April through December
Call for hours

More than three dozen culinary herbs sold as bedding plants or cut-your-own are grown at Herbs of Grace. They include eight types of basil, 14 varieties of mint, and sage, chives, thyme, oregano, rosemary, hyssop, lemon grass, lemon balm, tarragon, parsley, and sorrel. Also available are everlastings, dried or in arrangements.

San Jose

Clark's Greenhouse and Herbal Country
R.R. 1, Box 15B
(309) 247-3679
Open: Daily April and May
9:00 a.m.-4:00 p.m (from 1:00 p.m.-Sunday)
Other months weekend by appointment

Wilma Clark raises 167 varieties of herbs and 67 varieties of scented geraniums and other edible flowers, as well as everlastings. She sells the herbs and flowers fresh, dried, or as bedding plants. Bedding plants are available from April through June, and fresh herbs are available all year round. You may go into the gardens and cut your own herbs or buy them ready-picked. She also gives tours of her display gardens and teaches a few classes in herb gardening. She has a mail-order catalog from which she sells everlastings, herbs, and scented geraniums as either live plants or dried bunches. See the mail-order section for catalog information.

Shirley

Funks Grove Pure Maple Sirup
Box 41
(309) 874-3220 or 874-3360
Open: Mid-February through June or July

When Isaac Funk came to Illinois in 1824 he made maple sirup for his family the way the Native Americans had taught his pioneer ancestors to do so. In 1891, his grandson Arthur began making it to sell. Hazel Funk Holmes took over the operation and it was she who changed the spelling in syrup from "y" to "i." Contrary to the illiteracy it appears, Mrs. Holmes insisted on the "i" because her favorite dictionary defined *syrup* as sweet liquid made by adding sugar to fruit juice, and *sirup* as sweet liquid made by boiling down sap. Today, a billboard 15 miles south of Bloomington on I-55 tells travelers if any of the hundreds of gallons produced annually are available. The production of maple sirup begins in mid-February when thawing temperatures follow a hard freeze and the sap from maple trees begins to run. The earlier sap is the sweetest and needs the least cooking, so it is the lightest in color (amber) and the most preferred. The darker sirup, although less delicate in flavor, is still delicious. Maple sirup and maple sugar are sold from a shop near the Funk home. If you go there during the four- to -six week season that begins around mid-February, you will see the pails set out to catch the sirup, and perhaps a little of the sirup production. To get to

Funks Grove, take the McLean or Shirley exit off I-55 and follow the signs. The Maple sirup is also available mail-order. See *Mail-Order Shopping* on page 127.

Springfield

Bohlen's Orchard
217) 787-2854
Open: Mid-July through October
Call for availability

Brent Bohlen has a hobby that got out of hand and, as a result, those of us in the know can sample Thomas Jefferson's favorite apple, the apple that the Russian cosmonauts took into space, an apple that dates back 350 years, or any number of the 60 or so varieties that Bohlen grows at his family's orchard in Moweaqua and sells in Springfield. During apple season, he notifies his customers as the different varieties come off the trees, and customers pick up the apples at his home. Unlike apples grown at large, commercial orchards, his apples are picked when they are ripe and are sold at their peak. It's hard to believe that the apples in Bohlen's orchard are even distantly related to the bland, mushy apples we've had to settle for from the grocery store.

Bohlen's collection includes antique apples and other rare apples that have been in this country for some time but have not been available here, as well as apples that were developed for marketing by various agricultural experiment stations around the country. For a description of various apples see the Apple Chart on page 121. Some of the most popular or unusual varieties Bohlen grows are Arkansas Black, Blushing Golden, Calville Blanc, Cortland, Criterion, Empire, Esopus Spitzenburg, Fuji, Gala, Golden Russet, Granny Smith, Hudson's Golden Gem, Ida Red, Jonagold, Jonalicious, Jonamac, Kidd's Orange Red, Lady, Melrose, Mollie's Delicious, Mother, NY 428, Mutsu, Newtown Pippin, Northern Spy, Pink Pearl, Pitmaston Pineapple, Reinette Simirenko, Sweet

Sixteen, Spigold, Reinette Simirenko, and York Imperial. Incidentally, Thomas Jefferson's favorite apple was Esopus Spitzenburg, the Russian cosmonauts space apple was Reinette Simirenko, and the 350-year-old apple is Lady.

Briggs Orchard
405 Browning Rd.
(217) 544-1661
Open: August through Mid-October
Daily
8:00 a.m.-dusk

This 275-tree orchard near the airport has some apples as early as August. The season starts with such varieties as Ozark Gold and Gala. The orchard also grows Empire (a McIntosh cross), a huge Jonathan cross, Red Delicious, and Yellow Delicious.

Jacob's U-Pick Strawberries
R.R. 4
(217) 529-3478
Open: Mid-May to mid-June
Daily (call first to hear a recording about availability)
7:00 a.m.-4:00 p.m. or until picked-out

Jacob's eight-acre strawberry farm is primarily a U-Pick operation, but they will take some ready-pick orders if you call in advance. To get there, watch for the signs on Toronto Road, on the south side of Springfield.

Jeane's Strawberries
2802 W. Jefferson
(217) 546-7917
Open: Mid-May though the first week in June
Daily
7:00 a.m.-7:00 p.m.

This huge strawberry farm at the junction of Jefferson and Veteran's Parkway has 15 acres of strawberries. You can pick your own or buy them ready-picked. To buy them ready-picked, you go to the farm, take a number, and wait your turn for a picker to bring them in.

Jefferies Orchard (fruit and produce)
1016 Jefferies Rd.
(217) 487-7401
Open: Mid-April through October

The Jefferies family settled in Sangamon County in 1823 and has been on the same land a few miles past the airport on Rt. 29 ever since. The season begins in mid-April with asparagus that lasts until about the first week in June. U-pick strawberries begin about the last week in May and are available through mid-June when two weeks of U-pick Montmorency cherries and U-pick blueberries are usually ready. Fresh produce such as rhubarb, green beans, sweet corn, cabbage, cauliflower, broccoli, tomatoes, and eggplant are sold from the roadside stand as they are picked. Fall red raspberries are usually ready in September. The Jefferies grow Lodi, Red Delicious, Yellow Delicious, Jonathan, and Winesap as well as an apple known locally as "Russet Grimes," which is a medium-sized sweet russet apple.

Sabattini's Garden Center (produce)
R.R. 4, Hoechester Rd.
(217) 529-3620
Open: Mid-May through mid-November (or later)
Daily
Dawn until dusk

The Sabattini family begins selling fresh produce from their farm in mid-May. They specialize in corn, beans, variety peppers, and tomatoes but have other crops in smaller quantities. Here you can buy green onions, broccoli, sweet peas, cabbage, shallots, cauliflower, cucumbers, bell peppers, jalapeno peppers, gypsy peppers (large, yellow banana peppers), red peppers, purple peppers, striped peppers (green/yellow and yellow/red), four varieties of sweet corn, green beans, garlic, lima beans, butter beans, zucchini, summer squash, pumpkins, and more.

In the late summer and fall look for apples including Gala, Jonathan, Red Delicious, Golden Delicious, Winesap, and Grimes Golden. They also sell cider.

Robert Stevens (produce)
5859 N. Cotton Hill Rd.
(217) 529-1900
Open: June through mid-October
"All the time"

An added attraction to shopping at this 10-acre working farm it that you can see the exquisite blooming orchids that are casually displayed from Mrs. Stevens's collection of 1,500 orchid plants. Here the season starts with spinach and sweet peas. Later you can buy green beans, cucumbers, tomatoes, butter beans, lima beans, peppers, cabbage, potatoes, and sweet potatoes that last so long in the cupboard you'll wonder how old those shriveled ones in the grocery store must be!

Suttill's Garden (produce, fruit, bedding plants)
2201 Groth
(217) 744-9379
Open: Mid-March through Thanksgiving
Daily until Halloween when closed on Sunday
8:00 a.m.-6:00 p.m. (except 9:00 a.m.-4:00 p.m. Sunday)

A few blocks west of Dirksen, just off Ash, Ron Suttill sells fresh produce from his family farm, which has remained in Springfield for three generations while the city kept growing around it. Not only is the produce less expensive than at the grocery, but it is as fresh as can be--much of it is picked the same day. The season begins in March when Suttill starts selling bedding plants, including vegetables and flowers. As the season progresses you can buy green beans, spinach, cucumbers, tomatoes, sweet peppers, broccoli, cabbage, potatoes, sweet potatoes, turnips, corn, and squash, as well as a list of hard to find vegetables such as okra, Asian eggplant, Italian eggplant, lima beans, crowder peas, mustard greens, collard greens, tomatillos, and various hot peppers that he grows at the request of his regular customers who provide him with seeds.

Suttill also sells fruit. He grows ice-box melons, a basketball-sized watermelon with rind so thin it could never withstand commercial handling and flesh so sweet you'll never want to eat thick-skinned watermelon again. He also sells fruit from other farms and orchards. Cantaloupe, nectarines, peaches, plums, and apples are some of the fruits you can expect to find. You can dig your own mums, and if he hasn't yet picked the vegetable you want, and it's ready, you might be invited to go pick it yourself.

Vesper Taylor (honey)
97 Circle Drive
(217) 529-5929
Open; By appointment

Springfield's premier beekeeper is Vesper Taylor. When a swarm of bees descended upon a shopper's bicycle in a local parking lot, it was Taylor who was called to spirit the swarm away. When people who have allergies read that local honey will help them build a tolerance to pollen, they buy his honey in an attempt to relieve their symptoms. Or, when those of us who enjoy the taste of honey want some that is locally produced, we can buy it directly from him or at various berry farms, orchards, health food stores, and produce markets that sell it.

Taylor's bees produce two types of honey. The light amber-colored honey comes from locust trees and the sharper-flavored dark honey comes from wildflowers. Bees can travel up to 2½ miles for a nectar source and during peak season, can fill a hive in three days. According to Taylor, bees will not mix their nectar source in one hive. Taylor sells raw honey in liquid form or, as a novelty, in the wax honeycomb. To buy honey directly from him, call him to set up a time to visit and bring your own container.

Stonington

Schmidt Fruit Farm
R.R.1, Box 94
(217) 325-3333
Open: May through apple season
Call ahead for hours

Schmidt Fruit Farm has strawberries and apples. You can pick your own strawberries or buy them ready-picked. The orchard grows Red Delicious, Yellow Delicious, Jonathan, Ozark Gold, and Criterion apples. They are available beginning in August or September. Cider is available in the fall. The farm is located near Stonington, which is northeast of Taylorville.

Sullivan

Okaw Valley Fruit Farm
R.R. 2, Box 124
(217) 728-8269
Open: Memorial Day though mid-June (for strawberries) and mid-August until mid-October (for apples)
Daily
6:30 a.m.-7:00 p.m (1:00 p.m.-5:00 p.m. Sunday) strawberry season
9:30 a.m.-6:00 p.m. (1:00 p.m.-5:00 p.m. Sunday) apple season

This small fruit farm has three acres of U-pick or ready-picked strawberries, and 250 trees of apples of the following varieties: Red Delicious, Yellow Delicious, McIntosh, Granny Smith, Jonathan, and Rome. The 350 new trees that will start bearing in 1992 or 1993 include Gala, Blushing Gold, and

Winesap. To get there, go four miles north of Sullivan on Rt. 32 and two miles west.

Tallula

The Winkelmann Farm (maple syrup)
R.R. 1, Box 83
(217) 634-4224 or 632-3919

A few years ago Robert Winkelmann began tapping the maple trees on his land to make maple syrup so he could use the profit from the sale of the syrup to save for his children's college educations. In 1991 he produced all of 37 gallons of maple syrup. The maple syrup is light amber in color, delicate, fragrant, and absolutely ambrosial. It is available beginning in March.

The Winkelmann's also have a limited supply of blackberries and black raspberries in June. Call ahead for more information on the availability of maple syrup and berries and for directions to the farm.

Taylorville

Big "M" Berry Patch (produce, berries)
R.R. 3, Box 319A
(217) 824-6625 or 824-3289
Open: April through frost
7:00 a.m.-dusk

The Big "M" Berry Patch, a few miles southwest of Taylorville, grows asparagus, strawberries, red and black raspberries, corn, green beans, and tomatoes.

Asparagus is available in April and is ready-picked. You can pick your own strawberries from the six-acre patch or you can have them picked for you. They are ready to be picked beginning in May or June.

Big "M" has red and black summer raspberries that ripen in June just after the strawberries end. Also available are fall red raspberries. The summer red raspberries are a large-type berry, and the fall reds are a smaller, more intense, variety. They are available for U-pick or already-picked.

Trilla

Moran Orchard
R.R. 1
(217) 895-3408
Open: End of May or beginning of June through fall
Monday through Saturday (for strawberries) plus Sunday in the fall
8:00 a.m.-dark (7:00 a.m. for strawberry picking)

About 10½ miles south of Mattoon, you can pick your own strawberries in the spring, buy peaches, nectarines, and plums in the summer, and buy apples in the fall. The strawberry operation is U-pick only, but the rest of the fruit is sold from a building at the orchard. Peaches and nectarines are available from mid-July through August. Moran's has a variety of apples including Gala, Ozark Gold, Mollie's Red, Idared, Mutsu, Red and Yellow Delicious, Grimes Golden, Cortland, Jonathan, and Stamen Winesap. Cider is available after October 1.

White Heath

The Pontius Farm, Ltd. (berries)
P.O. Box 70
(217) 762-7714
Open: Daily
7:00 a.m.-5:00 p.m. (from 7:00 a.m. for strawberries and Sunday from noon)

The Pontius Farm has five acres of strawberries, 13 acres of blueberries, two acres of raspberries, and Concord grapes. The strawberries are ready around Memorial Day and are available for about two weeks. The blueberries are ready around the first of July and are available through mid-August. Both strawberries and blueberries are U-pick, with a few sometimes available ready-picked. The red raspberries are the fall variety that are ready around Labor Day and available until the first killing frost. Raspberries are U-pick only. Concord grapes are available at the end of August until the end of September. Be sure to call to hear a recording for the availability of berries. To get there take the White Heath exit off of I-72 and watch for signs.

Apple Chart

The variety of tastes and textures that apples provide is astonishing to people who have grown up eating Red Delicious as the standard. In central Illinois, we are lucky to have a number of growers who are branching out and trying new apple varieties. Locally grown apples provide us with a wonderful opportunity to taste apples at their best--fresh off the tree. Although some apples need to be eaten within weeks of picking for the best flavor, others improve with age or can be stored for months with no loss of flavor. This chart will tell you which apples are the best "keepers." Tasting different apples is great fun, so go ahead--there's a wealth of flavors for the trying.

*Arkansas Black-*As unusual in flavor as it is beautiful in appearance, this apple is such a dark red that it appears purple. It is too hard to eat when harvested but after a few months in storage the flesh is dense, not especially juicy, and has a slight almond flavor.

*Ashmead's Kernel-*This rather ugly golden-brown russet apple, according to Tom Vorbeck is "not for sissy palates." It is juicy, sugary, and has been grown for more than 200 years.

*Blushing Golden-*This is a popular, pretty yellow apple with a pink blush. It is similar to Golden Delicious but has more snap, is tarter, and is a better keeper.

*Braeburn-*A pretty new variety from New Zealand, this apple is crisp, sweet, and juicy and has an excellent flavor.

*Calville Blanc-*King Louis XIII grew this very pretty pale yellow apple, and it is still served for dessert in fashionable restaurants in France. It has an unusual sweet spicy flavor and has more vitamin C than an orange.

Chieftan-A cross between Jonathan and Delicious but sweeter than Jonathan and a better keeper than Delicious.

Criterion-This light yellow apple has a firm texture, a mild flavor, and is a good keeper.

Cortland-A McIntosh cross, this large apple has deep-red stripes and a soft texture.

Empire-This is an excellent tasting and very pretty apple. It is a cross between a Red Delicious and McIntosh and is crisp and juicy.

Esopus Spitzenburg-This antique apple was Thomas Jefferson's favorite. "Spitz" is a wonderfully flavored apple that is best eaten after a month or so in storage.

Fuji-A crisp, juicy apple, it is one of the world's fastest growing in popularity. It will stay crisp and juicy for months and has an excellent, sweet flavor.

Gala-This earliest of the sweet apples, Gala is quickly becoming one of the most popular apples in America. It is beautiful, with its yellow and pink skin resembling a peach, and is crisp, spicy, and very delicious--although not for those who like their apples tart.

Golden Russett-An antique apple that is sugary, fine grained, and juicy. It has a thin russett-colored skin that is not attractive but is an excellent keeper.

Granny Smith-This sweet-tart, pretty green apple helped change the way apples are produced and marketed in America. It is an excellent tasting, late maturing apple that keeps well.

Hudson's Golden Gem-This is the largest of the very good, crisp, sweet, juicy, but ugly russet apples.

Idared-For the best flavor you should store this deep red apple. It is sweet, spicy, and a good keeper.

Jonagold-A large pretty apple, this is a cross between a Jonathan and Golden Delicious. It is a sweet and popular apple, but it is not a good keeper.

Jonalicious-This popular apple is a relative of Jonathan but is larger, sweeter, juicier, and a better keeper.

Jonamac-This apple is a cross between a Jonathan and a McIntosh, and although not a good keeper, it has a good McIntosh flavor and can be grown well in Central Illinois. (McIntosh apples don't grow well here.)

Jonathan-An old apple, this is a red, sweet-tart apple that is used for cooking, eating, and cider making.

Kidd's Orange Red-This pretty and wonderfully flavored apple is a parent of Gala. It is the choice for those who like the spicy flavor and crisp texture of Gala, without the cloying sweetness.

Lady-A tiny flat apple that dates back 350 years in Europe. This apple is crisp, tart, and aromatic and is still used in Christmas ornamentation.

McIntosh-A sweet-tart apple that does not grow well in Central Illinois.

Melrose-This cross between Jonathan and Red Delicious is a better keeper than Jonathan and is especially good for baking.

Mollie's Delicious-An early, large red apple that has a better taste than Red Delicious.

*Mother-*This very good eating apple is aromatic, sweet, and juicy, but it is not a good keeper.

*Mutsu-*A wonderful, large, spicy, juicy apple that keeps well.

*Newtown Pippin-*This antique apple that Benjamin Franklin enjoyed is a classic. Crisp and delicious, it is an excellent keeper that develops its full flavor after months of storage.

*Northern Spy-*Bite into this apple and be taken back to the fall bonfires of your childhood--it is that good! It has complex flavors but is not particularly attractive, and it bruises easily.

*N.Y. 428-*This apple doesn't have a name yet because it is still in the experimental stage at the agricultural station in Geneva, New York. It has a sweet flavor and crisp texture.

*Ozark Gold-*This large crisp yellow apple is sweet and juicy and is a good keeper.

*Paula Red-*An early apple with a sweet-tart flavor.

*Pink Pearl-*This pink-fleshed apple with light-green skin is a bit tart and does not keep very well.

*Pitmaston Pineapple-*This small russet apple is very sweet and has the distinct flavor of honey and pineapple.

*Reinette Simirenko-*This yellowish-green slightly tart apple originated in the Ukraine and was taken into space by the Soviet cosmonauts.

*Spartan-*A cross between McIntosh and Newtown Pippin, this is a beautiful, dark red apple that is aromatic, juicy, crisp, and a better keeper than McIntosh.

Spigold-A huge, lopsided temperamental apple, it is worth the trouble to get it. Juicy, crisp, and having a complex spicy flavor, this is one of the truly great apples.

Sweet Sixteen-This new apple is a Northern Spy cross. It has a firm, crisp texture and an anise flavor.

Tydeman's Late Orange-This cross of Cox's Orange Pippin reaches its best eating quality around Christmas.

Winter Banana-This large, yellow apple with a pink blush is hard, crisp, aromatic, and has a mild flavor.

York Imperial-An antique apple with a wonderfully complex flavor and crisp texture, it is an excellent keeper.

Shopping for Morels

From the banks of the Illinois River and the small islands in the river, local mushroom fanciers bring in hundreds of pounds of morel mushrooms during mushroom season, usually from the second week in April through Mothers Day. Local lore tells of 10-inch mushrooms found in the area. The mushroom hunters, many of whom make their living off the river, sell their mushrooms through the local taverns. They are not cheap--anywhere from $8 to $15 a pound. If you are interested, call any of the taverns listed below. If they don't have any for sale, ask them who might.

Approach Inn Main St., Meredosia (217) 584-1838

Ben and Gen's Locust St., Eldred (217) 983-2346

County Line Lake Inn Chandlerville (217) 458-2733

Duke's Tavern Chandlerville (217) 458-2821

Leo and Bud's Tavern 600 E. 4th, Beardstown (217) 323-9754

Louie's Kampsville Inn Kampsville Ferry Landing, Kampsville (618) 653-4413

Southside Tavern Main St., Meredosia (217) 584-9905

Waterworth's 124 N. Plum, Havana (309) 543-9156

Mail-Order Shopping

Six central Illinois businesses allow you to shop by mail-- for yourself or for unique, locally produced gifts. There are apples from a list of more than 80 varieties, cow's milk cheese, goat's milk cheese, fine Belgium chocolates, herbs, and maple syrup. Some of the items are available seasonally and some are available year-round.

Applesource
R.R. 1, Box 94
Chapin 62628
(217) 245-7589

Applesource is a unique apple orchard that grows more than 100 varieties of apples. Its unique catalog business allows you, or the recipient of your gift, to sample the diversity of apple flavors. Applesource has a number of different boxes-- containing either one or two trays of apples--from which to choose. Perhaps the most interesting are the explorer pack and the sampler pack, which contain up to 12 different varieties of apples. For the more adventurous, there is a pick-your-own (PYO) box that allows you to choose the assortment. They come in a heavy, nicely decorated box and are available from the end of October until January. Call or write for a copy of the Applesource catalog.

The Arthur Cheese Company
P.O. Box 308
Arthur 61911
(217) 543-2166

The Arthur Cheese Company produces wonderful natural cheese. Its wonderful, creamy Baby Swiss has won both national and international U.S. Cheesemaker's Association competitions. Among other delicious selections from the 30 or so produced by the company are cheddar, smoked cheddar, Gouda, and low-fat Swiss. Please note: the award-winning Baby Swiss is called Danish Swiss on the price list. Cheese can be purchased by mail-order. A gift catalog is available on request. Call or write for a catalog and price list.

Clark's Greenhouse and Herbal Country
R.R. 1, Box 15B
San Jose, 62682
(309) 247-3679

Wilma Clark raises herbs, scented geraniums, and other edible flowers, as well as everlastings. She has a mail-order catalog from which she sells some of the everlastings, herbs, and scented geraniums as either live plants or dried bunches. For a copy of the catalog send $2.00.

Dietrich's Dairy
Route 1, Box 83
Fowler 62338
(217) 434-8460

Dietrich's Dairy is locally producing European-style goat cheeses costing half that of their French counterparts. The creamy French-style chevres are available in various sized logs: 4 oz., 8 oz., and 2 lbs. You can buy them plain or rolled in your choice of condiments: black pepper, onions and chives, dill and onion, or sweet basil. Dietrich's also makes its own unique Dietrich's Blue, an American version of Roquefort. It has the texture of Monterey Jack and the sharpness of a good tangy blue cheese. You can buy this special treat in a 6-lb. wheel or in a half wheel.

Funks Grove Pure Maple Sirup
Box 41
Shirley 61772
(309) 874-3220 or 874-3360

When Isaac Funk came to Illinois in 1824 he made maple sirup for his family the way the Native Americans had taught his pioneer ancestors to do. In 1891, his grandson Arthur began making it to sell. More than 100 years later, the family is still making maple sirup; sometimes 1,000 gallons a year! The production of maple sirup begins in mid-February when thawing temperatures follow a hard freeze and the sap from maple trees begins to run. The earlier sap is the sweetest and needs the least cooking, so it is the lightest in color (amber) and the most preferred. The darker sirup, although less delicate in flavor, is still delicious. Sirup is usually available from the first of March until June or July. You can buy Funks Grove maple sirup mail-order, while the supply lasts, by writing or calling for a catalog.

Rubens Chocolates
811 Oak St.
Danville 61832
(217) 442-0442 or 1 800 245-1514

Rubens chocolates are exquisite to behold as well as to taste. Handmade by Chris Thurston, a native of Belgium, they are prepared using fine Belgian chocolate and fresh cream, butter, fruit, and nuts. Thurston trained under a Belgian chocolatier and brought her skills with her when she moved to Danville. Her giandujas--classic, hazelnut-cream-filled chocolates--are sublime. Her truffles are rich, smooth, and creamy, and her honey caramels are like liquid gold. She makes two dozen varieties of chocolates that can be purchased mail-order in elegant gold boxes. Call or write for a copy of Rubens's beautiful brochure.

Seasonal Products Index

Some products are available only during specific months. This index tells you when they begin to be available and where you can find them.

February: maple syrup
April: morel mushrooms
May: asparagus, strawberries
June: blackberries, cherries, raspberries
July: blueberries
August: apples, fall raspberries, nectarines, peaches
September: Concord grapes, pumpkins
October: pecans

Apples

Arenzville, 85
Bloomington-Normal, 86
Brighton, 87
Carlinville, 89, 90
Champaign-Urbana, 91
Chapin, 92
Chatham, 93
Fisher, 98
Greenup, 99
Lincoln, 102
Mahomet, 102
Mail-Order, 127
Moweaqua, 104
New Berlin, 104
Springfield, 111, 112, 113, 114, 116
Stonington, 117
Sullivan, 117
Trilla, 119

Asparagus

Athens, 85
Brighton, 87
Buffalo Hart, 88
Chatham, 93
Fisher, 98
Lincoln, 101
Petersburg, 106
Pontiac, 107
Springfield, 113
Taylorville, 118

Blackberries

Arenzville, 85
Brighton, 87
Buffalo Hart, 88
Chatham, 94
Coffeen, 94
Fisher, 98
Tallula, 118